Environmental Law

A Practical Handbook

Environmental Law

A Practical Handbook

John Garbutt

Partner, Nicholson Graham & Jones, London

JOHN WILEY & SONS

Chichester • New York • Brisbane • Toronto • Singapore

First edition published 1992
Second edition published 1995
Reprinted August 1996

Published in the United Kingdom by John Wiley & Sons Ltd,
Baffins Lane, Chichester,
West Sussex PO19 1UD, England

National   01243 779777
International (+44) 1243 779777
e-mail (for orders and customer service enquiries):
cs-books@wiley.co.uk
Visit our Home Page on http:/ /www.wiley.co.uk
or
http:/ /www.wiley.com

British Library Cataloguing in Publication Data

A catalogue record for this book is available from the British Library

ISBN 0-471-95226-5

Typeset in 11/13pt Garamond by Mayhew Typesetting, Rhayader, Powys
Printed and bound in Great Britain by Biddles Ltd, Guildford and King's Lynn

Environmental Law
A Practical Handbook

John Garbutt has been a solicitor for 30 years. He is a Partner and Head of the Planning and Environment Unit at City solicitors, Nicholson Graham & Jones; has been employed in Local Government and subsequently was chief executive of both the waste management and industrial minerals divisions at Blue Circle Industries. He also set up and ran their environmental affairs office. He is a member of the CBI Minerals Committee and the Environmental Legislation Panel and has served on the Health and Safety Executive Advisory Committee on Major Hazards. He is a member of the UK Environmental Law Association speaking and writing extensively on environmental matters from a legal and managerial perspective.

For my father, one of that great body of solicitors whose dedication to their clients, great or small, is the strength of our profession.

Contents

Contents

Preface to the Second Edition

Nicholson Graham & Jones is a leading City of London law firm founded in 1858. Its strengths are in company law, litigation, tax, pensions and property but in recent years it has developed a number of specialisms of which the Planning and Environment Unit is one of the more recent.

Even if the reader has been cut off from civilisation for some time he or she could not have failed to notice the extent to which, on a world scale, concern with the environment and the use of land and resources has become a major issue. To the lawyer, this manifests itself in an unprecedented range of new legislative and government initiatives which bear down mostly on the polluter but also on every individual. The impact of these changes at international level on our clients and others led us to establish the Planning and Environment Unit. That its work load has increased significantly (there are now four full-time solicitors in the Unit) indicates the extent of client need.

Given the great trend in the law to increase the size of practices and to develop large specialist groupings it is sometimes easy to forget that the strengths of the professions rest on a national pattern of small to medium-sized practices whose partners and fee-earners need to have knowledge in many branches of the law. This book is aimed at them. It is also for the guidance of the in-house lawyer and the very wide range of practitioners in other professions, industry and commerce who now look for reasonably simple guidelines.

I have perceived that there is a need for a guide to the range of new and existing environmental law, designed to assist general practitioners, in particular with an overview of the present state of the law and to equip them to deal with questions and problems which will arise frequently, because almost every client will now have to face some responsibility to the environment and will need help. The format of the book is aimed to help to reduce the time which needs to be undertaken for research and which general practitioners and consultants can often ill afford. It is against this background that the work seeks to help and advise.

I would offer two main *caveats*. First, this is a handbook or short guide. It gives an outline of the law for busy practitioners but does not pretend to be a definitive treatise on the whole detail and minutiae relating to this rapidly expanding subject. Where appropriate, I have added signposts to further reading and study on specific aspects of the law. Second, the law relating to the environment is changing fast. Royal assent to the Environmental Protection Act 1990 was granted at the end of that year, but at the time of writing, the Act is not fully in force. Parts of the Act, notably Part I, come into force only by reference to specific industries and processes. It is important to make careful checks as to the applicability of the law as between these industries and processes.

The opportunity has been taken in this second edition to rewrite the chapters on water law and to update the sections on waste management, particularly to take into account the coming into force of most of the remaining Part II of the Environmental Protection Act 1990, bringing with it all the complexities of the Framework Directive on Waste and the new transfrontier shipment laws. A new section on contaminated land has been prepared and Appendix E on EC law has been updated. Part 3 contains a new section on the burgeoning rights of public access to environmental information. The law is as it is understood at 30 September 1994.

I owe some acknowledgements. I would like to thank my partners at Nicholson Graham & Jones for their positive help and support in promoting the concept of this book. I owe a debt to Lisa Dinsley and other colleagues who have word processed the whole volume with their typical willingness and skill.

John Garbutt
October 1994

Tables

Statutes

Statutory Instruments

European Secondary Legislation and Treaties

Introduction

"In Britain we have well-developed systems for controlling and regulating pollution. The Water Act 1989 and the Environmental Protection Bill of 1990 include measures to strengthen the powers and resources of the various inspectorates. The government favours strong pollution inspectorates with clear remits to impose high quality standards.
The objects are:

To make our air cleaner and safer;
To achieve further improvements in the quality of our water and in the state of the North Sea and our other coastal waters;
To establish the levels of emissions that our air and waters can safely tolerate, and set up control mechanisms based on that;
To maintain and strengthen when necessary, controls over pollution from industry, including farming, and over dangerous chemicals and other substances; and
To provide the necessary incentives to industry to improve their environmental standards and develop clean technologies."
This Common Inheritance: Britain's Environmental Strategy (White Paper, September 1990, Cm 1200).

This is a small quote from a very large White Paper but it provides the essence of HM Government's policy intentions for the protection of the environment. To judge from current expressions of the other political parties it does not seem likely that environmental policies will be materially different as a result of any change of government.

One of the political parties to have made very little progress in the UK (and to have declined in parts of Europe) is the "Green" party. No doubt in its early days its policies filled a vacuum, apparently because the major parties gave little obvious priority to the environment. In this they were well proved not to have measured accurately the mood of their electors but one suspects that the position has now been righted.

In volume and complexity, environmental legislation has now taken a quantum leap. The major new statutes, the Water Resources Act 1991 and the Environmental Protection Act 1990 introduce new concepts of responsibility and control in respect of which the lawyer, particularly the solicitor, will need to be well versed.

It is apparent that since all members of the human race are users of the main elements of the environment the legislation and policies concerning those elements will be bound to impact upon virtually every living soul. In a great many cases the impact will be sufficiently significant that the individual or organisation will require legal and other advice. New clients will be drawn not only from industry and commerce but from diverse occupations such as farming and forestry, hunting and fishing, finance and lending, transport and retailing, advertising and consumer affairs. The list seems endless.

Duties and liabilities so far as the environment are concerned will centre on a clear understanding, not only of the primary legislation but of the following other aspects.

(i)   Statutory instruments.
(ii)   Government circulars.
(iii) Other governmental statements of policy.
(iv)   Codes of practice, both from government and other agencies.
(v)   Orders and policies of other agencies such as the National Rivers Authority, HM Inspectorate of Pollution and the Health and Safety Executive.
(vi)   European Commission pronouncements, where, increasingly, the Brussels influence is being felt (see Appendix E).
(vii) Case law from Britain and elsewhere, particularly the European Court of Justice.

The role of the solicitor will be to keep his client abreast of:

(i)   the rights and duties in regard to environmental law;
(ii)   the prohibitions and permissions associated with the use of natural resources and the handling of waste and other matter;
(iii) the means by which authorisations, permissions and licences may be obtained;
(iv)   the proper application of government controls. In this regard the solicitor is responsible to protect his client from excesses of government agencies;
(v)   the civil and criminal law relating to the environment, the defences and penalties; and
(vi)   the rights of the individual to complain to the controlling agency or to take individual or "class" actions.

In short, the solicitor's duties and liabilities are to know, in reasonable detail, the law as it applies to his particular client and to ensure that that client is provided, first, with the protection to which he is entitled and, second, with the keys to unlock the gates to solutions to his environmentally related problems and difficulties.

The practitioner, therefore, must have, firstly, an understanding of the statutory and other law pertaining to the environment (see Part 1 of this book). Secondly, he will need an appreciation of the procedures to obtain authorisations and approvals (see Part 2). Thirdly, he will need a reasonable understanding of civil and other liabilities and the rights of his client to use the civil courts for redress (see Part 3). Finally, an understanding of European Community environmental policy and law is now crucial.

The consequences and influences on other parts of the law will be fully appreciated. Environmental law impinges, for example, upon company, commercial, litigation, property, health and safety and criminal sectors.

Nonetheless, there are difficulties.

(i) The legislation is now so extensive and complex that it is in danger of overtaking the average person's capacity to understand.

(ii) Hitherto, training both before and subsequent to qualification tends not to meet the advancing need for environmental advice.

(iii) It is a peculiarity of environmental law that there is a major intrusion of ministerial, local authority and other quasi-government agency policies. A compendium of knowledge of this usually intricate area is extremely difficult to secure.

(iv) The European factor, as previously referred to.

This book attempts to overcome some of these problems. It seeks to provide a general guide in handbook form to assist lawyers and others in a basic understanding of the burgeoning environmental law and to help the search for reliable advice. However, I should caution that this is only a general guide, and deals largely with the law and policy in England and Wales. It does not purport to be an exhaustive treatise on this wide subject. Readers will be guided to other material for a more detailed examination.

The first two parts of this book (Part 1, The Statutory Codes and Part 2, Applications for Approval) are mainly written by reference to the specific environmental medium or category of impact, for example water, air etc. In the case of noise, there being few examples at the present time where applications for approval are required, such application procedures are included in Part 1.

Part 1

The Statutory Codes

Contents of Chapter 1

Chapter 1
Water Abstraction and Water Pollution

Water abstraction

Introduction

Responsibility for control of water abstraction is now vested in the National Rivers Authority (NRA) under the Water Resources Act 1991. Abstraction was largely a matter for common law, but the Water Act 1945 imposed restrictions and some control on abstraction. It established a local organisation of water supplies, defining powers and duties of local authorities and water undertakers. However, until the advent of the Water Resources Act 1963 there was no comprehensive code of control of water resources management.

Water Resources Act 1963

The Water Resources Act 1963 (WRA 1963) established a sub-regional structure of authorities tending to be based upon the main river basins. For the first time a formal and comprehensive restriction on the abstraction and impounding of water was imposed, although exceptions were provided for, both in the Act and by subsequent regulations. Otherwise, from June 1965 abstraction of water was forbidden except by licence. The prohibition included not only abstraction direct from a surface supply, for example a river or lake, but also the construction of any well or borehole designed to withdraw water from underground (WRA 1963, s 23). In the main, exceptions were restricted to small abstractions (not exceeding 1,000 gallons) and abstraction from an inland water for an occupier of contiguous land for use on that land, either for domestic purposes or agriculture, other than spray irrigation. Similarly, abstraction from underground strata for domestic purposes was also excepted, but then further restricted by the Water Act 1989. Further exceptions permitted abstraction for the purposes of land drainage or to prevent interference with mining, quarrying, engineering, building or similar operations. The restriction did not prevent the transfer of water from one inland water to another by a navigation, harbour or conservancy authority, nor the abstraction for use on a vessel, for the purposes of fire-fighting or for test purposes.

Licence of right

Section 33 of WRA 1963 provided a special entitlement to a licence to abstract, known as the "licence of right". Such licence was granted automatically to any person who was entitled to abstract water from a source of supply in a river authority area as at the date that this part of the Act came into force, or had a record of five years' continuous abstraction. The provision was of particular value to major industrial abstractors, although an obligation to pay for such abstraction was established by Part V of the Act, now embodied in section 123 of the Water Resources Act 1991 (WRA 1991).

Impounding

The right to impound an inland water was restricted by section 36 of WRA 1963. Impounding includes the provision of a dam, weir or works for diversion. A licence to permit such works would be granted under section 36.

Appeals

There were provisions for an appeal against, or lack of a decision of, the water authority. The appeal was made to the Secretary of State for the Environment. The decision by the Secretary of State was final, save that the validity of the decision as a matter of law might be questioned by section 117 of WRA 1963.

Miscellaneous matters

Abstractions or impounding without licence or in contravention of conditions of a licence were offences (WRA 1963, s 49). There is an important additional benefit to the holder of a licence to abstract: not only is he protected from any challenge to his right to abstract (subject to compliance with the licence and payment of charges) but he also owns a protected right in the sense that the NRA is liable not to derogate from that grant. Such right is now preserved by section 60 of WRA 1991.

Water Act 1989

The Water Act 1989 (WA 1989) generated further significant changes to the water industry arising specifically from the Government's decision to privatise the water supply industry. However, excluded from the powers and responsibilities of the new water companies (generally having similar identities to their predecessors, the water authorities) was the regulatory function which now devolves to the NRA. The overall effect of this was that whilst the water companies remain the suppliers of water and sewerage services to individuals and organisations, regulatory control (*i.e.* the conservation and security of the proper use of water resources in England and Wales) is now for the NRA to manage. A significant consequence of the split of the responsibilities for operation and regulation is the avoidance of any conflict of interest between the commercial implications of supplying water and sewerage services and proper, objective regulation, particularly of the latter. The regulatory policy of the NRA appears to be much firmer than that demonstrated by the former water authorities, with a greater readiness to prosecute and effect policing, monitoring and long-term resource strategies.

In its impact on commerce and industry generally, WA 1989 did not significantly alter WRA 1963, except that abstractions for domestic and agricultural use were more closely limited. However, this had a major effect upon large agricultural water users such as fish farms, which were, for the first time, brought within the licensing requirements. However, a transitional provision allowed licences of right for abstractions made during a five-year period before 1 September 1989 provided that applications for licences were made within one year from that

11

date. As a concession to small generators of electricity (less than five megawatts) the abstraction of water for this purpose is not subject to charge.

Finally, in relation to water resources the Act provided a more detailed regime for the imposition of drought orders and for penalties for offences against such orders.

Water Resources Act 1991

The Water Resources Act 1991 (WRA 1991) was part of a general consolidation of water legislation by the UK Government and assembles previous extant provisions which established the powers and duties of the NRA particularly with regard to the protection of water resources. The other consolidating measures were the Water Industry Act 1991, controlling the supply of water and the provision of sewerage services by the privatised water companies, the Land Drainage Act 1991, concerning internal drainage boards, local authorities and their powers specifically in regard to land drainage and the Statutory Water Companies Act 1991, relating primarily to the private water companies which had existed by virtue of private acts of parliament in the nineteenth century and which are now also subject to the Water Industry Act 1991. Transitional and certain other arrangements are provided for in the Water Consolidation (Consequential Provisions) Act 1991. The consolidation legislation came into force on 1 December 1991.

Abstraction and impounding

Restrictions on abstraction and impounding are now to be found in Part II of WRA 1991 (ss 24 and 25 respectively).

Abstraction

As a general rule no person shall (i) abstract water from any source of supply or (ii) cause or permit any other person to so abstract any water except in pursuance of a licence granted by the NRA, and in accordance with the provisions of that licence. By the same token obstruction of any well, borehole or similar means by which water can be abstracted or even the extension of such facility, or the installation or modification of machinery or apparatus for abstraction is an offence. Penalties for abstraction or the other forbidden activities on summary conviction can result in a fine not exceeding the statutory maximum (presently £5,000) and on conviction on indictment to an unlimited fine. A "source of supply" is defined in section 221 of the Act to include any inland water (mainly rivers, streams, lakes or ponds, whether natural or artificial together with certain channels, creeks, bays and estuaries) and underground strata containing water. It should be noted that waters which are "discrete" (*e.g.* lakes, ponds or reservoirs or groups of them which have no connection with any other inland water) are not within the definition of source of supply.

Exceptions from requirement for licensing

There are a limited number of exceptions from the need for a licence to abstract water.

(i) Single abstraction of less than five cubic metres of water but not if such abstraction is part of an operation or series of operations during which more than that amount is abstracted.

(ii) An abstraction of 20 cubic metres, similarly limited provided that the quantity does not exceed 20 cubic metres. However, such abstraction requires the consent, as opposed to a licence, of the NRA.

(iii) An abstraction not exceeding 20 cubic metres per day from an inland water (see above) for use on contiguous land for domestic or agricultural purposes other than spray irrigation.

(iv) Abstraction from underground strata for domestic purposes not exceeding 20 cubic metres per day.

In some circumstances the rights to abstract small quantities, which are provided by section 27 of WRA 1991, may be curtailed by the NRA (s 28).

Section 29 offers further rights to abstract in special circumstances:

(i) in the course of or resulting from operations of land drainage;

(ii) to prevent interference with mining, quarrying, engineering, building or other operations (whether surface or underground) or to prevent damage to works resulting from the operations. This exemption applies even where the water abstracted is used for purposes of the operations (s 29(3)).

Section 26 lifts the restrictions on both abstraction or impounding where water is being transferred from one area of inland water to another in connection with operations carried out by a navigation authority, harbour authority or conservancy authority or in the case of impounding in the course of the carrying out of the functions of those authorities.

Restrictions on impounding

It is an offence to undertake or alter any impounding works at any point in any inland waters which are not "discrete" waters without a licence granted by the NRA and in accordance with the conditions of that licence.

"Impounding works" are defined in section 25(8) as including any dam, weir or other works in an inland water or any works for diverting the flow of any inland water in connection with the construction or alteration of such dam, weir or other works.

Exceptions to the requirement for a licence to impound include:

(i)   the rights in section 26 (see above); and
(ii)   generally, the construction or alteration of impounding works previously unauthorised by other legislation (s 25(5)).

Water pollution

Introduction

The main statutory responsibility for the prevention of water pollution in England and Wales now derives from WRA 1991, Part III which, from 1 December 1991, replaced WA 1989, by way of consolidation.

Earlier legislation

Prior to WA 1989 control of water pollution in England and Wales existed by virtue of provisions in the Control of Pollution Act

1974. This had modified what had amounted to the first comprehensive water pollution legislation in the Rivers (Prevention of
Pollution) Acts 1951 and 1961.

However, there remain some important remnants of earlier
provisions. The Public Health Act 1936 identifies as a statutory
nuisance (see p 83) ponds, ditches, etc which are prejudicial to
health or a nuisance, or silted-up water courses (s 259).

The above legislation related to the acceptance of effluent and
pollution into the existing network of sewers. In the meantime
preventative legislation relating to discharges to rivers etc was
developing through the Rivers (Prevention of Pollution) Acts 1951
and 1961. Control is largely now embodied in WRA 1991 which
provides the NRA with the closest and most complex system of
control of pollution of water so far devised. To some extent the
legislation arises as a consequence of EC directives (*e.g.* as to
purity of drinking water (see below).

Water Industry Act 1991

The Water Industry Act 1991 (WIA 1991), replacing by way of
consolidation the Public Health (Drainage of Trade Premises) Act
1937, provides the legal basis upon which the occupier of any
trade premises may, with the consent of the sewerage undertaker,
discharge his trade effluent into the local sewers. It is the
responsibility of the occupier of the trade premises to supply a
notice to the undertaker specifying the nature or composition of
the effluent, the maximum quantity to be discharged per day and
the highest rate of discharge. There is a right in the undertaker to
prohibit or regulate by conditions the nature, composition or
quantity of the effluent to be discharged. In the event of dispute
there is an appeal to the Secretary of State for the Environment
(ss 118 *et seq*).

The 1937 Act was substantially modified by the Public Health
Act 1961 in that it permitted conditions to be imposed on consents
and gave power to vary those conditions. Another effect of the
1961 Act was to widen the definition of trade premises so as to
include those used for agriculture or horticulture or for scientific
research or experiment. These modifications are now embodied in
WIA 1991.

Water Resources Act 1991

Important definitions

These are three elements to the approach of WRA 1991, which are, "controlled waters", "water quality objectives" and the attainment of those objectives.

Controlled waters are defined in section 104 as including lakes and ponds, rivers, estuaries, water in underground strata and certain coastal waters. Sections 82 to 84 impose on the Secretary of State a duty to classify, achieve and maintain the quality of controlled waters and to specify water quality objectives which it will be the responsibility of the NRA to achieve and maintain. The Secretary of State will retain an overall responsibility. What this means to business and the individual is that section 85 offences are committed if:

(i) any poisonous, noxious or polluting matter or any solid waste is caused or knowingly permitted to enter any controlled waters;

(ii) any matter other than trade effluent or sewage effluent is caused or knowingly permitted to enter controlled waters through discharge to a drain or sewer in contravention of a prohibition imposed by section 86;

(iii) any trade effluent or sewage effluent is caused or knowingly permitted to be discharged to any controlled waters or into the sea outside controlled waters; or

(iv) generally, any trade effluent or sewage effluent is discharged in contravention of section 86 from any building or plant onto any land or inland water.

Some difficulties have been experienced in the definition of "causing". There have been a number of cases (see *Wychavon District Council* v *NRA* [1993] 2 A11 ER 440; *NRA* v *Yorkshire Water Services Limited*; and *NRA* v *The Wright Engineering Company Limited* (both reported in (1993) *The Times*, 15 November)).

Section 86 gives to the NRA the power to serve a notice prohibiting any discharge or imposing any conditions on a continuing discharge.

Avoidance of the offence under section 85 is achieved provided that any consent is granted under the terms of section 88. This consent may be by various means, which include formal approvals under the Act itself, the Control of Pollution Act 1974 or Part I of the Environmental Protection Act 1990 (see the discussion on integrated pollution control at p 24).

Water protection zones and nitrate sensitive areas

A new concept within WA 1989, now in WRA 1991, relates to the pro-active powers contained in sections 93 and 94 (water protection zones and nitrate sensitive areas). Section 93 allows the Secretary of State (after consultation with the Minister of Agriculture) to prohibit or restrict the carrying on in a particular area of activities likely to result in the pollution of controlled waters. These are special powers which are made available to the Secretary of State to prevent or control the entry of any poisonous, noxious or polluting matter. The more specific power contained in section 94 is similar. The power here is exercised by the Minister of Agriculture in England and is expressly to prevent or control the entry of nitrates into controlled waters which results from the use of land for agricultural purposes. Both the Secretary of State and the Minister have taken powers to provide codes of good agricultural practice which have, as one of their objectives, a reconciliation of viable agriculture with the avoidance of pollution.

—

Contents of Chapter 2

Chapter 2
Air Pollution and Integrated Pollution Control

Introduction

Atmospheric pollution control has its roots in the long-established Alkali etc Works Regulation Act 1906, but was considerably modified by the Clean Air Acts 1956 and 1968 and the Control of Pollution Act 1974. Certain other modifications derived from the Health and Safety at Work etc Act 1974. Part I of the Environmental Protection Act 1990 (EPA 1990) will eventually replace the Alkali etc Works Regulation Act 1906. The EPA 1990 now represents the primary legislation relating to air pollution, although the Clean Air Act 1993 (replacing the earlier act of that name and the Control of Pollution Act 1974 continues to deal with certain miscellaneous air pollution events such as the prohibition of dark smoke from industrial or trade premises and requirements for standards for furnaces. However, the new requirements of EPA 1990 will be brought into force only gradually and, in the meantime the above provisions will continue to apply for existing processes. At the stage where a new or substantially altered process is proposed, EPA 1990 authorisation requirements will apply. So far as existing, unchanged processes are concerned, a legislative transition will take place over a period planned to extend to 1995. Enforcement of the legislation is primarily the responsibility of HM Inspectorate of Pollution (HMIP) (although direct policing is limited to the major industrial processes) and the local public health authorities will have the remaining duties.

The Alkali etc Works Regulation Act 1906

Processes are scheduled under the Alkali etc Works Regulation Act 1906. Scheduled processes are now set out in the Health and

Safety (Emission into the Atmosphere) Regulations 1983 (SI 1983/943) as amended by the Health and Safety (Emission into the Atmosphere) (Amendment) Regulations 1989 (SI 1989/319). The combined effect of the legislation and the regulations is to require registration of all works and processes set out in the Schedules to the 1983 and 1989 Regulations. Scheduled processes are required to be registered with HMIP and must comply with a requirement for "best practicable means" to prevent the escape of noxious or offensive gases. Certification is required on an annual basis and regular inspection takes place. Usually, for the major industries, proceedings may only be taken by HMIP, so that public health authorities' powers are restricted. However, nowadays many of the less significant processes, particularly those deriving from smaller and less "high-tech" industry, such as mineral works, now devolve directly to the public health authority for enforcement, thereby reducing the load placed on HMIP.

Clean Air Act 1993

The Clean Air Act 1993 (CAA 1993) replaces the Clean Air Acts 1956 and 1968. It makes an occupier of buildings emitting dark smoke guilty of an offence (sections 1 and 2). However, there are certain exemptions set out in section 1, and the prohibition does not apply to the emission of dark smoke caused by the burning of any matter prescribed in regulations made by the Secretary of State. "Dark smoke" is specifically defined in section 3(1) by reference to the Ringelmann Chart (*i.e.* more than 40% obscuration). However, the court is permitted, in certain circumstances, to conclude that smoke is or is not dark smoke even if there has been no comparison with the Chart. The offence may be committed from open sites.

Part II of the Act requires that new furnaces must, as far as practicable, be smokeless (section 4) and that there should be limits on rates of emission of grit and dust from furnaces (section 5). It is an offence to allow the escape of such materials and, furthermore, to install such a plant without notification to the local authority. The main popular feature of the Clean Air Act 1956, now replicated in Part III of CAA 1993, was to set in place provisions for local authorities to declare districts smoke control areas. This was in response to serious smoke-related air pollution problems in many cities in the 1950s. The effect of the establishment of a smoke control area is to prohibit the emission of any smoke, but subject to specific exemptions and limitations. However, certain authorised fuels are permitted to be burned, tending to be of the "smokeless' variety.

Part V of CAA 1993 (replacing Part IV of the Control of Pollution Act 1974) had little effect upon the earlier legislation so far as air pollution was concerned, except that it provided powers:

(i)   to regulate the composition of motor fuel so as to reduce air pollution (s 30);

(ii)   to regulate the sulphur content of furnace or engine oil so as to reduce air pollution (s 31);

(iii) to prevent cable burning except under proper conditions (s 33);

(iv)   to require information about air pollution for the purposes of publishing information to the public. There are certain protections in regard to the demand for information if to give it would prejudice commercial secrets, be contrary to public interests or be unduly costly and difficult to collect (Part V).

Health and Safety at Work etc Act 1974

Whilst the air pollution provisions of the Health and Safety at Work etc Act 1974 relate mainly to work place conditions, there are imposed general duties on persons in control of certain premises to prevent harmful emissions into the atmosphere (section 5).

Integrated pollution control and air pollution control by local authorities (EPA 1990)

The EPA 1990 was passed in November of that year. In relation to industrial processes which have a major potential for pollution, entirely new systems of control known as integrated pollution control will be instituted. Processes perceived as having less significance in pollution terms will be under the control of local authorities but only so far as air pollution is concerned. Processes and substances which are the subject of Part I of the Act are set out in the Environmental Protection (Prescribed Processes and Substances) Regulations 1991 (SI 1991/472).

The main regulations have been amended on a number of occasions by the Environmental Protection (Amendment of Regulations) Regulations 1991 (SI 1991/836), the Environmental Protection (Prescribed Processes and Substances) (Amendment) Regulations 1992 (SI 1992/614) and similarly named amendment regulations, numbered SI 1993/1749, SI 1993/2405, SI 1994/1271 and SI 1994/1329.

Integrated pollution control

Strictly speaking, the concept of integrated pollution control (IPC) is not a new one. There has always been a natural propensity in the systems of control through town and country planning, public health and pollution control to achieve the least offensive consequences of pollution by industrial and other activities. Thus, the Alkali Acts have progressively reduced atmospheric pollution in favour of recycling of gases and particulate matter leading to the disposal of the residue on land. Furthermore, the disposal of cooling waters to rivers and seas has been reduced in favour of discharges to atmosphere through cooling towers. Recycling and energy factors link to this concept.

What is integrated pollution control?

The IPC system arises through a scheme of authorisation, control and enforcement of processes capable of causing pollution of the environment. A process falls into this category if it releases to air, water or land, substances which are capable of causing harm to man or any other living organism supported by the environment (EPA 1990, s 1). The definition is exceedingly wide and likely to provide fertile ground for interpretative disputes in the courts and through the public inquiry procedures set up by the Act.

A process will not be caught by the IPC requirements until it is prescribed by the Secretary of State.

Preliminary

The power to prescribe processes is vested in the Secretary of State by section 2 of EPA 1990. The Secretary of State will, by regulations, prescribe any description of process in respect of which an authorisation is required under section 6. Regulations are intended to frame the description of the process by reference to characteristics, or the area, or other circumstances in which the process is carried on, or the description of the person undertaking it (see the Environmental Protection (Prescribed Processes and Substances) Regulations 1991 (SI 1991/472), as amended (discussed at p 103)).

The Secretary of State has assigned the more complex and highly technical processes for control by HMIP. However, a wide range of processes is intended to be designated for control by local public health authorities in England and Wales. To some extent the division of responsibilities is already established by virtue of the Alkali Acts and the Health and Safety at Work etc Act 1974, but the main difference in this area is that local authorities will now have prior authorisation duties which, hitherto, have not been required by the earlier legislation. A general list of these processes is set out in Appendices A and B.

It should be noted that by the Environmental Protection (Prescribed Processes and Substances etc) (Amendment) Regulations 1994 (SI 1994/1271), certain processes have been removed from control under Part I of EPA 1990 and others have been transferred from control by HMIP to that of local authorities, or vice versa.

Quality targets

Section 3 of EPA 1990 provides the basis for targets at which the Secretary of State will aim. The section will enable him to establish standards, objectives or requirements in relation to prescribed processes of particular substances. There are wide-ranging options for the Secretary of State, who would seem to have all necessary powers to:

(i)   limit the concentration, the amount or the amount in any period of a substance to be released from a prescribed process;
(ii)   limit any characteristic of the substance to be released;
(iii)   prescribe standard requirements for measurements;
(iv)   prescribe other standards or requirements as to any aspect of the process.

Associated with these wide powers is the additional power to make regulations applying different standards to different processes, industries, localities or circumstances. Section 3(5) establishes the right to secure a progressive improvement in the quality objectives and quality standards, and the Secretary of State's plans may be revised from time to time to accommodate such improvement.

Powers of HMIP and local authorities

The division of powers between HMIP and the local public health authorities is determined by section 4 of EPA 1990. In respect of HMIP there are effectively no geographical limits within England and Wales. Local public health authorities are responsible for processes carried on within their area but the functions applicable to such processes are exercisable in respect of air pollution and not to any other environmental medium (*i.e.* land or water). Special provision has been made in the case of mobile plant where the appropriate public health authority is that in whose area the person carrying on the mobile process has his principal place of business.

The Secretary of State has taken power under section 4 to transfer responsibilities normally exercised by a local authority to HMIP, but in these cases the limits of control (*i.e.* in respect of air pollution only) do not change (see the Environmental Protection (Prescribed Processes and Substances etc) (Amendment) Regulations 1994 (SI 1994/1271)).

The local authority

The local authority is defined in section 4 to mean (i) in Greater London, the London Borough Council, the Common Council of the City of London, the Sub-treasurer of the Inner Temple and the Under-treasurer of the Middle Temple; and (ii) outside Greater London, the district council and the council of the Isles of Scilly. There is a modification in those cases where, by the Public Health (Control of Disease) Act 1984, a port health authority has been constituted for any port health district. In this case, the responsibilities of Part I of the Act, normally assigned to the local authority, will be assigned to the port health authority.

Authorisations

Section 6 of EPA 1990 establishes a specific prohibition on any person carrying on a prescribed process (after the prescribed date) except by virtue of an authorisation granted either by HMIP or the local authority and in accordance with the conditions of that authorisation. The prescribed date by which an application for authorisation must have been made or granted is different depending upon the circumstances and the process in question.

Schedule 1 to the Act sets out some of the procedural requirements (see Chapter 8). The responsibility on the enforcing authority is either to grant the authorisation on the application made, subject to conditions, or refuse it. The enforcing authority is expressly forbidden to grant an application if it considers that the applicant will be unable to carry on the process so as to comply with the conditions which would normally be included in the authorisation.

Reviews of authorisations

It is to be noted that the enforcing authority will have a responsibility from time to time, but not less frequently than once in every four years, to carry out a review of the conditions of the authorisation. Indeed, this period may be changed by regulations made by the Secretary of State.

Applications for authorisations

Schedule 1 to EPA 1990 requires applications for authorisations to be made in such a manner as are prescribed in regulations (see the Environmental Protection (Applications, Appeals and Registers) Regulations 1991 (SI 1991/507). They will be accompanied by a fee and the usual requirement will be for advertisement, again as specified in regulations. The authority is entitled to all relevant information which must be supplied within a specified timetable and, in the event of the absence of information, the application may not proceed.

There are obligations on the enforcing authority to consult with prescribed persons and to consider any responses. Again, the regulations prescribe who will be the consultees. Besides those specifically consulted, all representations made within the time period are required to be considered by the authority in making a decision. There is a 28-day period for consultees and others wishing to make representations, starting respectively from the date on which notice of application was given or advertisement made.

In normal circumstances the enforcing authority has four months to make a decision on the application, or such longer period as may be agreed with the applicant. There are similar deemed refusal provisions as exist with planning applications.

Call-in powers

The Secretary of State may "call in" any application for his own decision and in those circumstances a local inquiry may be held whereby the applicant and the authority have a right of audience. The local inquiry must be held if either the applicant or the local authority require it. In the circumstances of "call in" the Secretary of State will apparently not make the decision himself but give directions to the authority as to whether or not to grant the application and as to the conditions to be attached to any authorisation.

Conditions of authorisations

Assuming that an authorisation is to be granted, section 7 of EPA 1990 is the operative provision for conditions of that authorisation. At this stage in the system there is a divergence between the IPC procedures for authorisation operated by HMIP and the air pollution control responsibilities of the local authority. They are, therefore, dealt with separately.

IPC

Section 7 of EPA 1990 sets out objectives (subs 2) as follows.

(i)   That in carrying on the prescribed process best available techniques not entailing excessive cost (BATNEEC) will be used for preventing the release of substances prescribed for any environmental medium into that medium or, where that is not practicable, reducing the release to a minimum and for rendering harmless any such substances which are so released and for rendering harmless any other substances which might cause harm if released into any environmental medium. The basic requirement on prescribed processes will be to employ BATNEEC. This definition is examined below (see p 32).

(ii) Compliance with any directions by the Secretary of State in pursuance of any obligations of the UK under European Community or international law relating to environmental protection.

(iii) Compliance with any limits or requirements and achievement of quality standards or objectives prescribed by the Secretary of State.

(iv) Compliance with any requirements of a plan for general improvement made under the provisions of section 3(5) which relates to total release limits, quotas etc.

(v) Where IPC applies (so that the process is designated for central control) and where it is likely to involve the release of substances into more than one environmental medium, the BATNEEC obligation extends to minimising pollution caused to the environment taken as a whole by the releases, having regard to the best practicable environmental option (BPEO) available as respects the released substances.

BPEO

In regard to IPC processes, the function of HMIP is to authorise only such processes which produce the optimum pollution control system (*i.e.* BPEO). Thus, discharges ultimately to land may be preferred as the least damaging, environmentally, when compared with discharges (*e.g.* to air and/or water). The implications of the BPEO system seem to be extremely wide and may well lead to *de novo* appraisals of process systems. Environmental assessments are to be an invariable requirement of any application for an authorisation made to HMIP and the testing of one method of environmental control against another will be part of these. The combination of BATNEEC and BPEO is seen as giving an impetus to the potential for recycling waste materials and effluent.

Local air pollution control

The objectives as described in section 7(2) of EPA 1990 are largely the same for local authority control except as regards the BPEO obligation. Since local authorities will be dealing only with relatively simple air pollution consequences of the processes under their control, the Government has not seen it as necessary to apply the integrated control assessments which will be the responsibility of HMIP.

Conditions

The enforcing authority must meet the above objectives in setting conditions of the authorisation. Additionally, it must take into account any directions given by the Secretary of State (EPA 1990, s 7(3)) and must impose any other conditions as may be appropriate. However, there is a prohibition against the imposition of any condition which has the purpose only of securing the health of persons at work. This is intended to avoid duplication of control already exercised under Part I of the Health and Safety at Work etc Act 1974.

Section 7(4) of EPA 1990 makes clear that there is implied in every authorisation a general condition requiring BATNEEC to be used to meet the objectives mentioned above.

Section 7(8) imposes further obligations in the form of conditions of an authorisation. An authorisation for carrying on a prescribed process may include conditions imposing limits on the amount or composition of any substance produced by or utilised in the process in any period and require advance notification of any proposed change.

Avoidance of duplication of controls

Section 28 of EPA 1990 contains some important provisions which seek to avoid conflict between different regimes of statutory control. These include:

(i)   that no condition may be attached to an authorisation to regulate the final disposal by deposit in or on land of controlled waste (this is now dealt with under Part II of the

Act and formerly by the Control of Pollution Act 1974). However, the enforcing authority must notify the waste regulation authority for the area where the process is to be carried on of the fact that the process involves the final disposal of controlled waste by deposit in or on land. It is to be noted that the authority to be notified is not necessarily that where the controlled waste is actually disposed of;

(ii) in circumstances where an authorisation is required under Part I and also under the Radioactive Substances Act 1960, and different obligations are imposed, the Part I provision will not be binding on the person carrying on the process;

(iii) in circumstances where the prescribed process designated for central control includes the release of substances into controlled waters under the Water Resources Act 1991, the NRA has certain powers of veto. These are that the enforcing authority must not grant an authorisation if the NRA certifies that the release to water will cause or contribute to a failure to achieve a water quality objective and in any authorisation granted, the NRA may require conditions to be imposed;

(iv) in the above circumstances, the NRA may also intervene to vary conditions of an authorisation if they see this as appropriate.

Allowing that the BPEO provisions give HMIP new statutory responsibilities in regard not only to air but also to water and land, it is difficult to escape the conclusion that the relationship with other authorities and their powers in respect of the other environmental media could be uneasy, at least in the early stages of the new IPC control system. Section 28 of EPA 1990 attempts to deal with the more obvious interface problems but, bearing in mind that there are bound to be conflicts between choices for disposal to different types of media, it seems more than likely that BPEO solutions will not always be universally acceptable to the NRA and the local authorities responsible for the disposal of waste on land. Industry might find itself caught in the cross-fire. However, proposals for a co-ordination of those functions in an environment agency should materially assist. The Government has announced the intention to establish an agency, which will effectively be an amalgam of the responsibilities of HMIP, the NRA and the waste regulation authorities. It is currently anticipated that a bill will be introduced to parliament during 1994/95.

BATNEEC

Section 7 of EPA 1990 is also the vehicle for defining the necessary and appropriate components of BATNEEC. In relation to a process, these include (in addition to references to any technical means and technology) references to the number, qualifications, training and supervision of persons employed in the process and the design, construction, layout and maintenance of buildings in which it is carried on. Section 7(11) places a duty on the enforcing authorities to have regard to any guidance issued to them by the Secretary of State for the purposes of this section, with particular regard to the techniques and environmental options which are appropriate for any description of prescribed process.

A general guidance note on the meaning of BATNEEC is set out in Appendix C. However, it will be noted that whilst some assistance is available in regard to the interpretation of best available techniques (BAT), the note is shy on the much more difficult element "not entailing excessive costs" (NEEC). A number of guides have now been issued by the Department of the Environment, notably "Integrated Pollution Control. A Practical Guide". The approach to NEEC will be likely to be different depending upon whether the process to be authorised is a new one or an existing one. It is to be anticipated that the courts will be called upon to assist with interpretation but, as a general guideline, it would seem that the presumption that BAT must be used, can properly be modified where the costs of applying those techniques would be excessive in relation to the nature of the industry and the environmental protection to be achieved. Economic considerations to be taken into account may be temporary or more prolonged, for example where a particular industry is in recession or suffering from individual economic difficulties. However, there is a limit to the extent to which overriding economic considerations can interfere with the requirement for BAT and this will depend upon the circumstances in each case.

Process guidance notes

The DOE and Welsh Office have issued a series of specific guidance notes on individual processes the subject of IPC. They are described as being based on the state of knowledge and understanding of such processes, their potential impact on the environment and the available control techniques at time of publication. The guidance is to be updated "regularly to reflect changes in knowledge and understanding". However, it has already been acknowledged that advances in technology may move faster than the revision of the guidance notes. Furthermore, the notes will not take into account individual process characteristics, for example location. This means that, on occasions, the choice of BATNEEC may not be fully identified by the extant guidance note hitherto relevant.

In addition to the process guidance notes, industry sector guidance notes IPR 1 to 5 have also been issued. These are more general assessments of five sectors of industry likely to be most affected by Part I of EPA 1990. They are fuel and power, metals, minerals, chemicals and waste disposal.

In relation to local authority air pollution control, further guidance notes have been issued, addressed to those local authorities who have responsibilities under Part I of the Act. There are five general guidance notes:

- GG1(91) – "Introduction to Part I of the Act";
- GG2(91) – "Authorisations";
- GG3(91) – "Applications and registers";
- GG4(91) – "Interpretation of terms used in process guidance notes";
- GG5(91) – "Appeals".

In addition, a range of process guidance notes have been issued covering those processes which are designated for local control.

All up-to-date guidance notes, relating both to IPC and local authority control, are obtainable from HMSO.

Fees and charges

A scheme of fees and charges is prescribed by the Secretary of State and section 8 of EPA 1990 provides for an updating of the scheme from time to time. Charges are imposed for (i) applications for authorisations (ii) variations and (iii) annual "subsistence".

The Secretary of State has made and undated separate charging schemes for HMIP and local systems of authorisation. The overall aim is that the system of fees and charges shall be self-sufficient by reference to the expenditure attributable to authorisations.

A failure to pay a charge renders an authorisation liable to revocation.

Transfer, variation and revocation

Transfer

An authorisation may be transferred on a change of any authorised holder. The responsibility to notify the enforcing authority is on the transferee, who must give notice of the fact within 21 days. From date of transfer the transferee takes on all the obligations of the authorisation and the conditions (EPA 1990, s 9).

Variation

Sections 10 and 11 of EPA 1990 lay down procedures applying where variation of conditions of authorisations are required to be made. An enforcing authority may vary an authorisation at any time and must do so if this is required by, for example, a change of circumstances in the conditions laid down by section 7.

Variation by enforcing authority

The procedure is triggered by the service under section 10 of EPA 1990 of a variation notice on the holder of the authorisation, which must specify the variations decided upon and the dates on which these variations are to take effect. The notice must also require the holder of the authorisation, within a specified period, to identify to the authority what action (if any) he proposes to take in response to the variation. A holder may be required to pay a fee, again within a specified period. In the circumstances where the enforcing authority is of the opinion that the variation will involve a substantial change in the process, the opinion must be notified to the holder and such holder will be required to advertise the change.

"Substantial change" is defined in section 10(7) as being " a substantial change in the substances released from the process or in the amount or any other characteristic of any substance so released". A power has been taken for the Secretary of State to give directions to identify what constitutes a substantial change. The term is discussed in specific IPC process guidance notes and, for local authority controlled processes, in paras 47–52 of General Guidance Note GG1(91) "Introduction to Part I of the Act" (see p 33).

Variation by holder of authorisation

The procedure for variation where the holder wishes to make any relevant change in the process is slightly different. It is to be noted that the requirements of section 11 are dictated by any need to make a "relevant change" in the prescribed process. This is defined as "a change in the manner of carrying on the process which is capable of altering the substances released from the process or of affecting the amount or any other characteristic of any substance so released".

In the case of a relevant change, the holder must:

(a) notify the enforcing authority; and
(b) request a determination of the following matters, viz:
    (i) whether the proposed change would involve a breach of any condition of the authorisation;
    (ii) if there is no breach, whether the authority would be likely to vary the conditions of the authorisation as a result of the change;
    (iii) if it would involve a breach, whether the authority would consider varying the conditions of the authorisation to enable the change to be made;
    (iv) whether the change would involve a substantial change in the manner in which the process is being carried on.

If the enforcing authority decides that no substantial change has taken place but that a variation of the authorisation should follow, the holder must be notified of the variation to be considered and the holder must then apply for such variation to enable him to make the proposed change.

Alternatively, if the enforcing authority decides that a proposed change would be a substantial one then the same procedure follows but, in addition, the holder must advertise the change in the prescribed manner.

On receiving the application for variation, the enforcing

authority may refuse the application or vary the conditions as it thinks fit and, in the latter case, must serve a variation notice on the holder of the authorisation. An appropriate fee will be applied here.

Further information on variation procedures is set out in General Guidance Note GG1(91) relating to local authority controlled processes.

Revocation of authorisation

Revocation of an authorisation is also available to an enforcing authority by virtue of section 12 of EPA 1990. The authority would deal with this where it has reason to believe that an authorised process had not been carried on for at least a period of 12 months. Twenty-eight days' notice of revocation must be given, but there is a power to withdraw the notice or vary the date at the discretion of the enforcing authority.

Enforcement

Powers of enforcement include the right to serve enforcement or prohibition notices.

Enforcement notice

These notices flow from contravention of any condition of an authorisation or the authority's anticipation that contravention is likely. The notice is required to specify that the authority believes that the condition is contravened or about to be contravened, must identify the matters representing the contravention and the steps that must be taken to remedy, as well as the period within which action must be taken. The Secretary of State may give directions here (EPA 1990, s 13).

Prohibition notice

The prohibition notice is a more serious matter and arises where the enforcing authority believes that an authorised process involves an imminent risk of serious pollution of the environment. Contravention of a condition of an authorisation is not a condition precedent. This notice must state the authority's opinion, specify the risk involved in the process and the steps that must be taken to remove it, as well as the period within which action is to be taken. Additionally, the notice must direct that the authorisation shall, either wholly or as to the extent specified in the notice, cease to authorise the carrying on of the process. This situation persists until the notice is withdrawn. The notice may, if it applies to part only of the process, impose conditions in carrying on the remaining part. Powers of direction are again available to the Secretary of State. Once the enforcing authority is satisfied that the steps required by the notice have been taken, it may serve notice withdrawing the prohibition notice (EPA 1990, s 14).

Appeals

Section 15 of EPA 1990 deals with rights of appeal in respect of Part I of the Act in the following circumstances:

(a)   on refusal of the grant of an authorisation;
(b)   on receipt of an authorisation with unsatisfactory condition;
(c)   on refusal of a variation;
(d)   on revocation of an authorisation;
(e)   on receipt of a variation notice;
(f)   on receipt of an enforcement notice;
(g)   on receipt of a prohibition notice;

In all cases, the appeal is to the Secretary of State.

The procedure for an appeal in each case requires the Secretary of State either to refer the matter to a person appointed by him for the purpose or to delegate the decision to an appointee. This procedure appears to be similar to that now applied in respect of planning appeals. The appeal will be required to be advertised and, if either party to the appeal so requests, a hearing (as opposed to an inquiry) shall be held. Part of this hearing or all of it may be held in private as the "inspector" decides.

For further information on procedures, see the Environmental Protection (Applications, Appeals and Registers) Regulations 1991 (SI 1991/507), regs 9–14.

Appeal powers of the Secretary of State

The powers of the Secretary of State in determining an appeal under (a) to (d) above extend to:

(a) affirmation of the decision;
(b) direction to the enforcing authority to grant the authorisation or to vary;
(c) quashing of unsatisfactory conditions; and
(d) quashing of any revocation.

Except in respect of the affirmation of the decision, directions may be given as to the appropriate conditions to be attached.

In the case of an appeal against a variation, enforcement, or prohibition notice ((e) to (g) above), the Secretary of State may either quash or affirm the notice and in the latter case he may do this either in the original form or with modifications.

Whilst in some cases an appeal will have the effect of suspending any revocation of an authorisation, this will not apply where a variation, enforcement or prohibition notice has been served.

Powers of inspectors

Inspectors appointed either by the Secretary of State or the local authority have a wide range of powers to administer and enforce the legislation (EPA 1990, s 17). These are exercisable in relation to premises (i) on which a prescribed process is or is believed to be carried on, and (ii) to premises on which a prescribed process has been carried on (whether or not the process was a prescribed process when it was being carried on), the condition of which is believed to be such as to give rise to a risk of serious pollution of the environment.

The powers of the inspector are:

(i) to enter at any reasonable time where there is an immediate risk of serious pollution and to take with him any duly authorised persons, including a constable if serious obstruction is anticipated, and any equipment or materials relevant to the power of entry (*i.e.* measuring equipment etc);
(ii) to make an examination and investigation;
(iii) to require premises or anything in them to be left

undisturbed so long as is reasonably necessary for examination or investigation;

(iv) to take measurements, photographs and other records as well as samples;

(v) to require the dismantling of any article or the testing of any substance where such have been thought to be likely to cause pollution of the environment and to take possession if necessary;

(vi) to require information from any relevant person as well as records;

(vii) to require any person to give facilities and assistance within that person's control and responsibility;

(viii) any other power conferred by regulations.

Protection of process operators and others

Enshrined in section 17 of EPA 1990 are various protections. For example, the power to dismantle equipment or subject substances to tests may not be undertaken without giving the opportunity for the person in charge of the premises to be present and in these circumstances the inspector is obliged to consult with all appropriate persons to ascertain dangers in the action which he proposes. The taking away of any equipment or sample requires the inspector to give notice to the responsible person or leave conspicuously a notice sufficiently identifying what was taken away and, where practicable, leaving a sample.

In so far as anyone has given information to an inspector, that information is privileged and not admissible in evidence in any subsequent proceedings. Furthermore, there is no right in an inspectorate to compel the production of any document which can be the subject of legal professional privilege.

Emergencies

Section 18 of EPA 1990 deals with the circumstances where the inspector has reasonable cause to believe that there is imminent danger of serious harm caused by an article or substance which he finds on any premises. He has power to seize the article or substance and cause it to be rendered harmless. However, before he may do this he is required to separate a sample and give it to a responsible person at the premises in question. The sample must be marked in a manner sufficient to identify it. Furthermore, as soon as possible after seizure and the rendering harmless of the article or substances a written report must be prepared by the inspector (and signed) identifying the circumstances. A copy of the report must go to the responsible person and to the owner of the article or substance. Service on the owner is satisfied if the inspector cannot reasonably ascertain the name or address, by service on the responsible person.

Information

Section 19 of EPA 1990 provides for the obtaining of information and is in two parts. In the first part the Secretary of State may, by notice in writing to an enforcing authority, require information about the discharge of its functions. In the second part, the Secretary of State or any of the enforcing authorities may require any person to give information as may be specified in a notice which the authority thinks it reasonably requires.

Offences

The offence provision is section 23 of EPA 1990. Offences arise if any person:

(a) fails to comply with the requirements of authorisations under section 6;
(b) fails to give notice under section 9 (transfer of authorisation);
(c) fails to comply with an enforcement or prohibition notice;
(d) fails without reasonable excuse to comply with the requirements of an inspector or prevents another person from doing so;
(e) intentionally obstructs an inspector in the exercise of his duty;
(f) fails without reasonable excuse to comply with a notice requiring information;
(g) makes a false or misleading statement;
(h) intentionally makes a false entry in any record required to be kept under a condition of an authorisation;

(i)   forges or uses an authorisation with intent to deceive;

(j)   falsely pretends to be an inspector;

(k)   fails to comply with a court order made under section 26 (see below).

Penalties are substantial, on summary conviction up to £20,000 and on indictment to an unlimited fine or imprisonment for up to two years, or both. Additionally, there is a right for the enforcing authority to go to the High Court if the proceedings in the lower court, for failure to comply with a prohibition notice or enforcement notice, are inadequate (s 24).

Supplementary powers are available under section 26 where there is a conviction for an offence under section 23(1)(a) – failure to obtain authorisation or comply with conditions, and section 23(1)(c) – failure to comply with any enforcement or prohibition notice. In addition to any punishment, the court may also order steps to be taken to remedy the offence but only if those steps are within the power of the offender to remedy. Furthermore, by section 27, HMIP, but apparently not the local authority, can obtain the authorisation of the Secretary of State to take steps to remedy harm and to recover the cost from the offender.

Standards of proof

Section 25 of EPA 1990 has an effect upon the normal standards of onus of proof. In circumstances where proceedings are taken against a person for failure to use BATNEEC it is for the accused to prove that no better available technique not entailing excessive cost was appropriate.

Further, the absence of an entry in a record required to be kept is admissible as evidence that the condition relevant to the record has not been observed.

Publicity

Public registers of information are required to be kept by section 20 of EPA 1990. In respect of prescribed processes, the following information needs to be registered as appropriate by HMIP and the local authority:

(i)   applications for authorisations made to the authority;

(ii)   authorisations granted or in respect of which the authority has functions under Part I;

(iii)   variation, enforcement and prohibition notices issued by that authority;

(iv)   revocations of authorisations effected by that authority;

(v)   appeals;

(vi)   convictions (as may be prescribed);

(vii) information obtained or furnished in pursuance of conditions of authorisations or under any provision of Part I;

(viii) directions given to the authority by the Secretary of State;

(ix)   any other matters as prescribed.

Local authorities (but not port health authorities) are also required to maintain in their register prescribed particulars of appropriate information contained in the register kept by HMIP as it relates to the carrying on in the authority's area of prescribed processes for which the HMIP has the responsibility.

Registers must be made available for inspection by the public free of charge. On payment of a reasonable charge, copies of entries may be taken (s 20(7)). Further particulars required to be kept in a register are prescribed by the Environmental Protection (Applications, Appeals and Registers) Regulations 1991 (SI 1991/507), reg 15.

Confidentiality

Some information may be excluded from the register but the register must make this clear. Exclusions arise under sections 21 and 22 of EPA 1990 in cases where the Secretary of State is satisfied that the information would affect national security. Furthermore, by section 22 no information relating to the affairs of any individual or business may be included in a register without the consent of the individual or business if it is commercially confidential and not specially required to be included in the register (see below). Information will only be regarded as commercially confidential if the authority so determines or if the Secretary of State determines after an appeal. Section 22(7) is important in that it gives to the Secretary of State the right to override commercial confidentiality if, in his view, the public interest requires that information to be included. Commercial confidentiality only lasts for four years, unless the supplier of the information requests a further exclusion and the authority must then decide whether or not that is the case. Commercial confidentiality arises if publication would prejudice the commercial interests of the individual or person to an unreasonable degree.

See also, as to national security and confidential information, the Environmental Protection (Applications, Appeals and Registers) Regulations 1991, (SI 1991/507) regulation 7.

Contents of Chapter 3

Chapter 3
Waste on Land

The legislative framework

Until the coming into force of Part II of the Environmental Protection Act 1990 (EPA 1990) (see p 53 below), the main legislative provision appropriate to the control of waste on land was the Control of Pollution Act 1974. However, there are other provisions of which the following may be appropriate in certain circumstances.

Public Health Act 1936

These provisions relate mainly to powers for the local public health authority to abate nuisances and/or to require an owner or occupier of premises to remove noxious matter, manure etc in an urban district (ss 79–80). Procedures are based upon the statutory nuisance provisions of the Act and are now replaced by Part III of EPA 1990 (see p 83).

Section 259(1) of the 1936 Act specifies that the definition of statutory nuisance for the purposes of Part III of that Act includes:

"(a) any pond, pool, ditch, gutter or water course which is so foul or in such a state as to be prejudicial to health or a nuisance;

(b) any part of a water course not being a part ordinarily navigated by vessels employed in the carriage of goods by water which is so choked or silted up as to obstruct or impede the proper flow of water and thereby to cause a nuisance, or give rise to conditions prejudicial to health. However, in regard to this paragraph there is a proviso that nothing in the sub-section shall be deemed to impose any liability on any person other than the person by whose act or default the nuisance arises or continues."

Public Health Act 1961

Section 34 of the Public Health Act 1961 provides a power to the local authority where, on any land in the open air in their area, there is any rubbish which is seriously detrimental to the amenities of the neighbourhood. In these circumstances the local authority may take steps for removing the rubbish in the interests of amenity. A necessary pre-condition to action is that notice must be served on the owner and occupier of the land stating the steps proposed to be taken by the local authority and the particulars of counteraction available to the person upon whom the notice is served. That person and any other person having an interest in the land may, within 28 days from the service of the notice, either serve a counter-notice on the local authority stating that he intends to take those steps himself or appeal to the magistrates' court on the grounds that the local authority was not justified in concluding that action should be taken under the section or that the steps proposed to be taken are unreasonable.

Section 34(3) goes on to provide that the local authority is required to take no further action in the matter unless the person who served the counter-notice fails, within the local authority's interpretation of a reasonable time, to begin to take the steps indicated in the notice or fails to make adequate progress to completion.

The definition of "rubbish" is dealt with in section 34(5) and includes rubble, waste paper, crockery and metal and any other kind of refuse (including organic matter), but does not include material accumulated for, or in the course of, any business or waste deposited in accordance with a disposal licence in force under Part I of the Control of Pollution Act 1974.

Control of Pollution Act 1974

The Control of Pollution Act 1974 (COPA 1974) brought into force a new system of control of waste disposal. With certain subsidiary legislation this remained the appropriate and current Act for 20 years but is now replaced by EPA 1990, Part II, which came almost fully into force on 1 May 1994. The incineration and other treatment of waste is also the subject of Part I of EPA 1990 (see Chapter 2).

The definition of "waste"

Waste was defined by section 30(1) of COPA 1974 as including:

(a) any substance which constituted a scrap material or an effluent or other unwanted surplus substance arising from the application of any process; and

(b) any substance or article which required to be disposed of as being broken, worn out, contaminated or otherwise spoiled

but did not include a substance which was an explosive within the meaning of the Explosives Act 1875.

It should be noted that for the purposes of offences under Part I of COPA 1974 "waste" was interpreted by reference to the person disposing of the material. Therefore, an occupier usually needed a licence for the disposal even of topsoil from a building site and could have been convicted of an offence of tipping this material on another's land without a licence (*Long* v *Brooke* [1980] Crim LR 109).

For the purposes of specific controls under COPA 1974 "waste" had a complicated definition, with three separate subdivisions.

"Controlled waste" under the Act meant household, industrial and commercial waste or any such waste. Three separate definitions were contained in section 30(3) as follows:

(a) household waste consisted of waste from a private dwelling or residential home or from premises forming part of a university or school or other educational establishment or forming part of a hospital or nursing home;

(b) industrial waste consisted of waste from any factory within the meaning of the Factories Act 1961 and any premises occupied by a body corporate established by or under any enactment for the purpose of carrying on under national ownership any industry or part of an industry or any undertaking, excluding waste from any mine or quarry;

(c) commercial waste consisted of waste from premises used wholly or mainly for the purposes of a trade or business or the purposes of sport, recreation or entertainment excluding:

    (i) household and industrial waste;

    (ii) waste from any mine or quarry and waste from premises used for agriculture within the meaning of the Agriculture Act 1947; and

(iii) waste of any other description prescribed for the purposes of this paragraph.

Powers were taken under section 30(4) for the Secretary of State to modify these definitions by reference to a specific type of waste. Some modifications were secured by the Collection and Disposal of Waste Regulations 1988 (SI 1988/819) and the Control of Pollution (Landed Ships Waste) Regulations 1987 (SI 1987/402).

Offences

The unlicensed disposal of controlled waste was an offence (COPA 1974, s 3) and was regarded as of sufficient seriousness that the worst cases could attract terms of imprisonment of up to five years and/or unlimited fines. The offences extended to:

(i)   depositing controlled waste on any land or causing or knowingly permitting the deposit; or
(ii) the use of any plant or equipment or causing or knowingly permitting such use in the disposal of controlled waste or dealing with controlled waste.

There was a second level of contravention which attracted serious penalties. This arose where the waste in question was poisonous, noxious or polluting, was deposited on land in a way likely to give rise to an environmental hazard and was left there, leading to the reasonable assumption of abandonment or disposal.

Licences

Disposal of controlled waste required a licence (COPA 1974, s 5) issued in England by the county council and in Wales by the district council (although other arrangements existed for London and the metropolitan authorities). The waste disposal authority was bound to grant the application (provided that it was in order) unless rejection was necessary for the purpose of preventing pollution of water or danger to public health. A planning permission for the activity must have existed under the Town and Country Planning Act 1990 or its predecessors before a disposal licence could be granted. The licence would impose a series of conditions (s 6). The Secretary of State for the Environment sponsored publications and codes of practice for guidance of the controlling authorities and licensees. (See various waste management papers obtainable from the Department of the Environment/HMSO.) Licences and conditions thereof could be varied and revoked, transferred and relinquished (ss 7 and 8).

Administration of licensed sites

Supervision of licensed activities was the responsibility of the authority issuing the licence (COPA 1974, s 9(1)). The authority had a duty (i) to take the steps needed so that the licensed activities did not cause pollution of water or danger to public health or become seriously detrimental to the amenities of the locality affected by the activity and (ii) to ensure that the conditions of the licence were complied with.

Enforcement powers

In order to perform the above duties there was power for an officer of the authority duly authorised in writing to take emergency steps and, if necessary to do so, to carry out work on the relevant land and on any plant or equipment to which the licence related (COPA 1974, s 9(2)). By section 9(3) any expenditure incurred as a result of taking the above-mentioned action could be recovered from the holder of the disposal licence, or, if that licence had been revoked or cancelled, from the person who last held the licence. However, the holder or last holder could escape responsibility for payment if he showed either that there was no emergency requiring any work or that the expenditure was unnecessary.

Further enforcement powers appeared in section 9(4) in circumstances where the disposal authority concluded that a condition of the licence was not being complied with. Whilst this was an offence punishable under section 3 and/or section 6(3), nonetheless it was open to the disposal authority to serve on the licence holder a notice requiring him to comply with the condition within a time-scale specified. Failure to comply with the condition as directed entitled the disposal authority to revoke the licence, again within a time-scale specified in the notice.

Appeals

Appeals lay to the Secretary of State for the Environment:

(i)   where an application for a disposal licence or modification had been rejected;

(ii)   against the conditions of a disposal licence;

(iii) against the terms of a modification of conditions of a disposal licence;

(iv)   against the revocation of a disposal licence (COPA 1974, s 10).

Procedure on modification

In circumstances where there was an appeal against modification of conditions of a disposal licence or against its revocation, a decision of the waste disposal authority was held in suspension until the appeal was dismissed or withdrawn (COPA 1974, s 10(2)). However, there were exclusions to this provision (s 10(3)) which arose where:

(i)   the notice was served in pursuance of section 7 (variation and revocation) or section 9(4)(b) (revocation after failure to comply with notice to comply with a condition); and

(ii)   the authority included in their notice a statement that in their opinion it was necessary for the purpose of preventing pollution of water or danger to public health that the suspension of revocation provisions should not apply.

If this notice had been included then the waste disposal licence remained varied or revoked until the decision on appeal of the Secretary of State was made. However, there was an interim provision (s 10(3)) which allowed the holder or former holder of the relevant licence to apply to the Secretary of State to determine that the authority had acted unreasonably in including such a statement in their notice. If the Secretary of State agreed with that assertion the suspension was lifted at the end of the day upon which the Secretary of State's determination was made and until such time as the appeal itself was determined. Furthermore, the holder or former holder of the licence was entitled to recover compensation from the authority in respect of any loss suffered by him in consequence of the statement. Disputes as to compensation were required to be determined by arbitration (see the Arbitration Act 1950).

Local authority site approvals

Section 11 of COPA 1974 applied where the land accommodating the disposal operation was occupied by the disposal authority itself. Special procedures then applied to protect the interests of, *inter alia*, the NRA and the public.

Special wastes

By section 17 of COPA 1974 powers were taken by the Secretary of State to impose a special regime of control in respect of dangerous or intractable waste. In pursuance of this section the Secretary of State has made the Control of Pollution (Special Waste) Regulations 1980 (SI 1980/1709). These regulations deal with a special system of control in respect of waste which is dangerous or difficult to dispose of. Special wastes are defined in the regulations. The regulations control the duties of carriers and disposers, importers and exporters and impose a system of ancillary consignment notes which must accompany the waste from its place of production to point of disposal. Whilst the regulations remain in force at present, the statutory basis for their successors will be section 62 of EPA 1990.

Environmental Protection Act 1990

Part II of EPA 1990 came almost fully into force on 1 May 1994. The whole of COPA 1974, Part I has been repealed and replaced by the 1990 Act. As such, the replacement represents a major overhaul of the powers and responsibilities of COPA 1974.

There is little change in administration. The same authorities which are waste disposal authorities under COPA 1974 are, largely, waste regulation authorities within the meaning of EPA 1990 (s 30(1)). Special arrangements exist in Greater London and the metropolitan counties. However, the operational powers of the authorities to dispose of waste themselves are brought to an end. The Act establishes a regime whereby the authorities in question have been required to form or participate in forming waste disposal companies (*i.e.* separate entities from the local authority from which they derive); alternatively, they may use the private sector or a combination of both.

Unauthorised depositing, treatment or disposal of waste

Except in relation to household waste on a domestic property and other special cases prescribed by the Secretary of State for the Environment, it is an offence (EPA 1990, s 33) to:

(i)   deposit controlled waste or knowingly cause or knowingly permit controlled waste to be deposited in or on any land unless a waste management licence authorising the deposit is in force and the conditions of that licence are complied with;

(ii)   treat, keep or dispose of controlled waste or knowingly cause or knowingly permit controlled waste to be treated, kept or disposed of in or on any land or by means of any mobile plant except in accordance with a waste management licence;

(iii) treat, keep or dispose of controlled waste in a manner likely to cause pollution of the environment or harm to human health. "The environment" is defined in section 29 as including land, water and the air, and "pollution of the environment" is defined as resulting from the release or escape into any environmental medium from the land on which the waste is treated, kept or deposited or the fixed plant by means of which waste is treated, kept or disposed of. The definitions also relate to mobile plant in the same way as applied to fixed plant. "Harm" is defined in section 29(5) as meaning harm to the health of living organisms or other interference with the ecological systems of which they form part and, in the case of man, includes offence to any of his senses or harm to his property.

Waste management licence

Generally speaking the definitions of "waste" and "controlled waste" were intended to be similar to those applying to COPA 1974, but EPA 1990 did contain more detail (see section 75).

However, the definition of "waste" in the EC Framework Directive on Waste has had a significant effect upon the Government's intentions. It has now indicated in Circular 11/94, "Environmental Protection Act 1990: Part II: Waste Management Licensing: The Framework Directive on Waste", that it will be necessary to repeal the existing definition of "waste" in section 75(2). Pending the introduction of the legislation, the Government has decided that only those substances or objects which are waste as defined in the Directive should be subject to the controls applying to the collection, transport, storage, recovery and disposal of waste. This has been provided by modifications to Part II of EPA 1990 by regulations (see the Waste Management Licensing Regulations 1994 (SI 1994/1056), which came into force on 1 May 1994).

It follows from the above that most activities associated with handling of waste will now require a waste management licence. However, some activities, prescribed by regulation 16 of the Waste Management Licensing Regulations 1994 are excluded from the requirement for a licence because they are already the subject of other control regimes. It should also be noted that the 1994 Regulations prescribe an extensive list of waste management activities which are exempt from the need for a licence. These are dealt with in regulation 17 of, and Schedule 3 to the Regulations. However, many of the exceptions are conditional, frequently because they require the consent of the occupier of the land in question. Furthermore, registration of exempt activities with the waste regulation authority is required (see reg 18 of the Regulations).

Duty of care as respects waste

Not only is there a prohibition on unauthorised depositing, keeping, treatment or disposal of waste (EPA 1990, s 33) but a new duty of care is imposed by section 34. The duty of care extends to any person who imports, produces, carries, keeps, treats or disposes of controlled waste or, as a broker, has control of such waste. The duty extends to the taking of all such measures which are applicable to that person in his capacity and which are reasonable in the circumstances:

(i)   to prevent any contravention by any other person of section 33;

(ii) to prevent the escape of waste from his control or that of any other person; and

(iii) on the transfer of waste, to secure that this is only to an authorised person or to a person authorised for transport purposes and that there is transferred a written description of the waste to enable such other persons to avoid contravention of section 33 and to comply with the duty to prevent the escape of waste (see above).

Generally speaking, the duty of care responsibilities do not apply to domestic property and the household waste produced there.

Authorised persons

"Authorised persons" are defined in section 34(3) of EPA 1990 as comprising:

(i) a waste collection authority;

(ii) the holder of a waste management licence under sections 35 or 5 of COPA 1974 (now repealed since 1 May 1994);

(iii) a person authorised by the Secretary of State under section 33(3);

(iv) a registered carrier of controlled waste under Control of Pollution (Amendment) Act 1989 or a person exempted by regulations under section 1(3) of that Act (see below).

Code of practice

The Secretary of State has published a code of practice giving practical guidance on the discharge of duty of care. The code of practice is admissible in evidence, particularly in deciding whether an offence has been committed under section 34(6) of EPA 1990 (see below).

The duty of care requirements of the Act came into force on 1 April 1992.

Offences

Sections 33 and 34 of EPA 1990 contain provisions relating to offences as follows:

By section 33(6) the unauthorised depositing, treatment or disposal of waste without a licence or in contravention of a condition of that licence is an offence, although certain defences are available under section 33(7). Proceedings may be brought for a summary conviction or on indictment, the penalties being greater in the second case. In relation to special waste (*i.e.* certain dangerous or intractable waste – see section 62), penalties on conviction on an indictment extend to two years' imprisonment.

A failure to comply with the duty of care provisions of section 34 can also attract penalties on conviction either summarily or on indictment (s 34(6)).

Special waste

The Secretary of State has taken powers under section 62 to provide by regulations a special regime of control in respect of special waste. Meanwhile COPA 1974 and the Control of Pollution (Special Waste) Regulations 1980 (SI 1980/1709) continue to apply.

Non-controlled waste

Section 63 of EPA 1990 contains powers for the Secretary of State to bring under control certain waste deriving from the agricultural and mines and quarries industries.

Publicity

The EPA 1990 includes new duties on waste regulation authorities to maintain registers containing a range of public information. This will relate particularly to information about:

(i) current or recent licences;
(ii) current or recent applications for licences;
(iii) applications and notices relating to the modification of licences, notices relating to the revocation or suspension of licences or imposing requirements on holders;
(iv) appeals;
(v) certificates of completion (see p 118);
(vi) convictions;

(vii) other matters relevant to the responsibilities of holders and the authority.

The contents of the register are prescribed by regulation 10 of the Waste Management Licensing Regulations 1994 (SI 1994/1056).

Exclusions from a register

By section 65 of EPA 1990 and regulation 11 of the 1994 Regulations, certain information may be excluded from a register with the sanction of the Secretary of State if it would be contrary to the interests of national security. The Secretary of State has taken powers to secure the exclusion of other information and section 66 allows certain confidential information of a commercial nature to be excluded under certain circumstances. However, there are restrictions on the extent to which commercial information may be excluded.

Imminent danger of serious pollution

The Act provides for action to be taken by inspectors either appointed by the Secretary of State or by the waste regulation authority. By section 70, an inspector has power to enter on any premises where he has reasonable cause to believe that an article or substance is a cause of imminent danger of serious pollution of the environment or serious harm to human health. There are powers to seize and to render harmless. There are also provisions requiring samples to be given to a responsible person at the premises and for the inspector to be responsible for a written report of the circumstances. Obstruction of an inspector is an offence dealt with either summarily or on indictment.

Control of Pollution (Amendment) Act 1989

The Control of Pollution (Amendment) Act 1989 took effect contemporaneously with section 34 of EPA 1990 (duty of care). It is an Act which attempts to render much more difficult the carriage of waste and the subsequent disposal of that waste in a manner falling far short of legal requirements. Following a number of unhappy examples which occurred, particularly in the 1980s, including dangerous fly-tipping, Parliament decided (on a private members' measure) that additional controls were necessary.

Transport in controlled waste without registering

Section 1 of the 1989 Act makes it an offence for any person, not a registered carrier of controlled waste and in the course of business or otherwise with a view to profit, to transport any controlled waste to and from any place in Great Britain. There are certain limited exceptions, which may be extended by the Secretary of State by regulations.

Registration

The Controlled Waste (Registration of Carriers and Seizure of Vehicles) Regulations 1991 (SI 1991/1624) require registration of persons with the waste regulation authority as carriers of controlled waste. Such registers will be available to the public and will include information about applications and certain other details.

Carriers of waste require a registration certificate, a copy of which must be kept on each vehicle and must be produced to an officer of the local authority or to the police. Registrations may be refused or revoked in circumstances where the applicant, or holder, or anyone associated with him has been convicted of a relevant offence or is regarded by the authority as undesirable. Appeals against refusal of registration etc are provided by section 4 of the 1989 Act.

It should be noted that in cases of an offence a warrant may be granted for the seizure of any vehicle involved in illegal waste disposal.

The transfrontier shipment of waste

Following the implementation in the United Kingdom of EC Regulation 259/93/EC on the supervision and control of shipments of waste within, into and out of the European Community, the

Department of the Environment has issued a Circular 13/94 on the subject. The EC Regulation came into force on 6 May 1994 and, coincidentally, the Transfrontier Shipment of Waste Regulations 1994 (SI 1994/1137) were issued by the Secretary of State.

The legislation gives effect to various conventions, including the Basel Convention on the control of transboundary movements of hazardous waste and their disposal. The EC Regulation covers the transfrontier shipment of virtually all waste. The UK Regulations replace those which were approved in 1988 (SI 1988/1562).

The new system is based on "prior informed consent", which requires notification to all the relevant controlling authorities of the despatch, destination and transit arrangements for any waste. Different rules apply as between disposal and recovery.

Control of industrial major accidents hazards

In some cases waste transfer stations and hazardous waste incinerators may be subject to the Control of Industrial Accidents Hazards (Amendment) Regulations 1994 (SI 1994/118).

Contents of Chapter 4

Chapter 4
Hazardous Substances

Introduction

This chapter deals with hazardous substances. This is a diverse subject, treated as such by the legislature. There is a wide variety of statutes dealing either wholly or in part with activities giving rise to hazardous substances and a regime of control for circumstances where escape and serious emergency might occur. This chapter does not deal with radioactive substances, a special subject which is not appropriate for a book of this type. Furthermore, a certain amount of the legislation has application mainly in the context of health and safety at work and has only tangential relevance to environmental conditions outside the place of work. However, certain parts of the Health and Safety at Work etc Act 1974 relate both to workplace and external environments and are dealt with in the following notes, by reference to appropriate subsidiary legislation.

Food and Environment Protection Act 1985

Part I of the Food and Environment Protection Act 1985 (FEPA 1990) relates to the contamination of food and entitles the appropriate minister (usually the Minister of Agriculture, Fisheries and Food) to make emergency orders where there has been or may have been an escape of substances:

(i) likely to create a hazard to human health through human consumption of food; or
(ii) which are or may be in the future derived from anything which is or may become unsuitable for human consumption. A range of activities that may be prohibited in a specific area is set out in Schedule 1 to the Act.

Practitioners will be familiar with the procedures which were last used extensively as a consequence of the Chernobyl incident in 1986. More recently, contamination of feeding stuffs orders were made in 1990 when there were fears of contamination of imported animal feed by the escape of lead.

Section 1 of FEPA 1985 makes it an offence to contravene an emergency prohibition, but certain actions may be approved by the appropriate minister under section 2 (see Chapter 10). Provided that the required consent has been given and that any conditions have been complied with, no offence is committed under section 1.

The section also provides the appropriate ministers with power to give directions to prevent human consumption of food where it is believed to be unsuitable and there is a blanket power to do all that is necessary for expedience. A failure to comply with a direction or the act of causing or permitting another to do so is an offence (s 2).

Investigating and enforcement officers are provided with wide powers by sections 3 and 4.

Pesticides

Part II of FEPA 1985, also gives to the enforcing ministers powers to make regulations:

(i)   to protect the health of human beings, creatures and plants;
(ii) to safeguard the environment;
(iii) to secure safe, efficient and humane methods of controlling pests; and
(iv) to provide information on these subjects.

These powers are effected by regulations. The powers include rights to impose prohibitions, approve pesticides for specified uses, require consent to anything contrary to a prohibition and to review generally. Powers of seizure are also provided. For regulations made under the Act see the Control of Pesticides Regulations 1986 (SI 1986/1510).

Codes of practice and enforcement

Sections 16 and 17 of FEPA 1985 provide for codes of practice to be set up by ministers. In this regard they are advised by the

Advisory Committee on Pesticides (see the Control of Pesticides (Advisory Committee on Pesticides) (Terms of Office) Regulations 1985 (SI 1985/517)). Section 19 spells out the enforcement powers of inspectors giving wide powers of enforcement, entry and direction.

Some powers have been modified by the Pesticides (Fees and Enforcement) Act 1989, but any authorisations granted before that Act are not affected.

Penalties for offences

Section 21 of FEPA 1985 specifies the penalties applicable to the offences under the Act. It is to be noted that directors and other officers of bodies corporate can be made personally liable. A general defence of due diligence is available under section 22. An employee and others may have the opportunity of sheltering behind this provision.

Planning (Hazardous Substances) Act 1990

The additional controls contained in the Planning (Hazardous Substances) Act 1990 (P(HS)A 1990) came into force on 1 June 1992. They adapt the town and country planning development control regime, which derived originally from the insertion into the Town and Country Planning Act 1971 of a new system of control authorised by the Housing and Planning Act 1986, Part IV. However, consolidation of the Planning Acts has now resulted in the Planning (Hazardous Substances) Act 1990. Until the 1986 Act, a system of control of operations and uses dealing with or resulting in hazardous substances was largely lacking as part of the development control system. This was because the definition in the Planning Acts of "development" was so wide that it gave freedom so that new hazardous uses and products could often be introduced, for example to a major factory operation, without any further planning consent being required. Whilst the Health and Safety at Work etc Act 1974 controls did exist, the powers of the executive were limited so far as planning control was concerned.

The overall effect of P(HS)A 1990 is that the keeping of any hazardous substances on, over or under land, beyond small quantities, will require consent of the hazardous substances authority (*i.e.* usually the London boroughs, the district councils in metropolitan counties and the district planning authorities elsewhere).

The Planning (Hazardous Substances) Regulations 1992 (SI 1992/656) set out the procedure when dealing with applications for consent. The procedures are similar to those relating to planning control.

Definition of "hazardous substance"

This is not specifically defined in P(HS)A 1990 but is defined in the Regulations (above).

Control is effected by the identification in the Regulations of the types of hazardous substances which are caught by the Act and the amount which is controlled ("the controlled quantity"). These are set out in Schedule 1 to the Regulations. Certain exemptions are prescribed by regulation 4. Procedures for express consent are set out in Part III of the regulations and forms are prescribed.

Deemed consent

Under section 11 of P(HS)A 1990 transitional provisions applied in those circumstances where hazardous substances have been present on the site for 12 months before the Act came into force. A claim for a deemed consent must be made within a period of six months from commencement date.

The procedures for claiming a deemed consent are in Part IV of the Regulations.

Enforcement, publicity and fees

These matters are dealt with respectively in Parts V, VI and VII of the Regulations. A hazardous substance contravention notice may be served by the authority under section 24 of P(HS)A 1990. This is in addition to other enforcement powers, including revocation or modification of the consent. Rights of appeal are available.

Offences

By section 23 of P(HS)A 1990 a contravention of hazardous substances control is an offence where either there is no hazardous substances consent for the presence of controlled substances or there is a breach of the conditions of that consent. The penalty on summary conviction is a fine not exceeding £20,000, and on indictment is an unlimited fine.

Circular

The Department of the Environment has published Circular 11/92, "Planning Controls for Hazardous Substances" which provide further guidance on the operation of the Act and the Regulations.

Environmental Protection Act 1990

There are two parts to the Environmental Protection Act 1990 (EPA 1990) which have a relevance to hazardous substances and the like.

Genetically modified organisms

A new system of control is established by Part VI of EPA 1990, specified by section 106 as having the purpose of preventing or minimising any damage to the environment which may arise from the escape or release from human control of genetically modified organisms. An "organism" is defined in section 106 to mean any acellular, unicellular or multicellular entity (in any form) other than humans or human embryos. Unless the context otherwise requires the term also includes any article or substance consisting of or including biological matters. That term is also defined in section 106.

An organism is "genetically modified" if any of the genes or other genetic material in the organism have been modified by means of an artificial technique (to be prescribed) or are inherited or otherwise derived through any number of replications from genes or other genetic material (from any sources) which was so modified.

Damage to the environment

Section 107 of EPA 1990 specifies that damage to the environment (*i.e.* land, air, water or any of those media) is caused by the presence in the environment of genetically modified organisms which have (or of a single such organism which has) escaped or been released from a person's control and are (is) capable of causing harm to the living organisms supported by the environment. A specification of the capability of causing harm is also provided in section 107.

General controls

Sections 108 *et seq* of EPA 1990 describe the powers of control available to the Secretary of State for the Environment, which he will exercise by regulations. In general, there is a prohibition against importing or acquiring, releasing or marketing any genetically modified organisms without a risk assessment and notice to the Secretary of State. A registration and consent system is established by the Act.

Section 109 indicates general duties of a person relating to importation, acquisition, keeping, release or marketing of organisms.

Enforcement

Powers of enforcement exist in section 110 (prohibition notices) and sections 111–112 of EPA 1990 which relate to the requirements and procedures for consents (see Chapter 10).

Offences

A wide range of offences is set out in section 118 of EPA 1990, relating mainly to failure to comply with the above procedures. It is noteworthy that by section 119 the onus of proof in certain circumstances is shifted to the accused, particularly in regard to the techniques used to comply with consent obligations and monitoring.

Publicity

By section 112 of EPA 1990 the Secretary of State is required to maintain a register giving a range of information concerning notices, directions, prohibition notices, applications for consent etc. Information may be excluded in certain circumstances on grounds of national security, potential damage to the environment or (subject to certain conditions) commercial confidentiality.

The Genetically Modified Organisms (Contained Use) Regulations 1992 (SI 1992/3217) and the Genetically Modified Organisms (Deliberate Release) Regulations 1992 (SI 1992/3280) provide detailed controls. Certain exemptions from the requirement to carry out risk assessments are to be found in the Genetically Modified Organisms (Contained Use) Regulations 1993 (SI 1993/15).

Environmental Protection Act 1990, Part VIII

The "miscellaneous" part of EPA 1990 contains various powers available to the Secretary of State to deal with hazardous and similar substances. These include:

(i) power to prohibit or restrict importation, use, supply or storage of injurious substances or articles. The power permits the Secretary of State to impose prohibitions and restrictions to prevent pollution of the environment or harm to human health or the health of animals or plants. Contravention results in penalties including imprisonment and fine (s 140);

(ii) the Secretary of State may also make regulations enabling him to obtain information about potentially hazardous substances (s 142). The specified purpose which is the basis for the demand for information is the potential for causing pollution of the environment or harm to human health.

Contaminated land

Substantial areas of contaminated land exist throughout the United Kingdom, particularly in the industrial regions. The industries of coal, iron and steel and other metals have left a severe legacy of extensive environmental harm and public danger. This can often affect ground and surface waters, leading to the abandonment of potential resources or extensive treatment. The health and safety of employees and members of the public generally can be prejudiced by poisonous residues and gases.

Section 143 of EPA 1990 was intended to enable the Secretary of State to establish registers of contaminated land to be kept by local authorities. However, during a number of consultation exercises it has become clear that practical difficulties attend the making and maintaining of registers, such that in March 1993 the Secretary of State announced that it was no longer intended to bring section 143 into force. At the same time, he set in train a further study which has resulted in the consultation paper, "Paying for Our Past". This discusses a wide range of issues pertaining to contaminated land, including liability, the need for rationalisation of existing legislative arrangements, standards to which clean-up should be pursued and strategy for proceeding to a programme of clean-up.

The existing legislation

There is no lack of powers available to both Central and Local Government to secure clean-up.

(i)   Part I of EPA 1990 gives HM Inspectorate of Pollution wide powers to impose conditions on authorisations (see Chapter 2). These powers seem to be sufficiently extensive to prevent ongoing pollution and possibly to require clean-up.

(ii) Part II of EPA 1990 enables waste regulation authorities both to require clean-up of contamination through conditions of a waste management licence and to refuse to allow the surrender of that licence because the condition of the land continues to offer the potential of pollution or harm to human health (see Chapter 3).

(iii) Contaminated land can be a statutory nuisance. Under Part III of EPA 1990 environmental health authorities have powers to require abatement of nuisance and/or the execution of works.

(iv) The National Rivers Authority has powers under the Water Resources Act 1991 to control and remedy pollution from contaminated land in circumstances where it is a threat to controlled waters.

(v) Powers are also available to the Health and Safety Executive under the Health and Safety at Work etc Act 1974, sections 21 and 22 and by the Town and Country Planning Act 1990, section 215, where the local authority may serve notices requiring the remedying of the condition of land adversely affecting the amenity of a locality.

All these powers offer to the regulator the opportunity to bring proceedings against the polluter landowner/occupier as the case may be. Coupled with this are powers for the regulators themselves to enter the land to carry out necessary works, recovering the cost from the person responsible.

Planning Policy Guidance Note PPG 23, "Planning and Pollution Control", published by the Department of the Environment, contains a section on contaminated land.

Contents of Chapter 5

Chapter 5
Noise

Introduction

Until the Noise Abatement Act 1960, the control of noise rested largely upon the nuisance provisions of the Public Health Act 1936. Otherwise, control was exercised, albeit uneasily, under the town and country planning system. The incidence of complaints of noise has been steadily increasing over the past 20 years or so, despite an overhaul of the legislation set out in the Control of Pollution Act 1974. This Act remains the significant statutory provision relating to noise and the Environmental Protection Act 1990 (EPA 1990) has not materially modified this. However, EPA 1990, Part III is now the main provision relating to statutory nuisance procedures (see Chapter 6).

Legislation dealing with specific circumstances may be found in the Civil Aviation Act 1982 (nuisance by aircraft) and the Motor Cycle Noise Act 1987 (which limits the supply of certain exhaust systems). A wide variety of regulations relating, for example, to noise insulation grants for property in the hinterland of major airports, codes of practice for ice cream van chimes, burglar alarms, model aircraft etc, should be noted.

The Noise and Statutory Nuisance Act 1993 empowers a local authority to impose restrictions on the operation of loudspeakers in streets and audible intruder alarms. The Act also amends EPA 1990, Part III in relation to statutory nuisance procedures (see Chapter 6).

Control of Pollution Act 1974

Duties of local authorities

Section 57 of the Control of Pollution Act 1974 (COPA 1974) is specific in that periodical inspections by local authorities are required to be made to decide upon the exercise of powers concerning noise abatement zones (see below).

Control of noise on construction sites

Noise from construction sites represents a major cause of complaint to local authorities and others. Sections 60 and 61 of COPA 1974, therefore, present a remedy. Under section 60, the local authority may serve a notice specifying how the works are to be carried out. The notice may specify which plant and machinery is to be used or not used, the hours to be worked and the level of noise. The local authority is required to take into account any relevant codes of practice established under section 71 (see the Control of Noise (Code of Practice for Construction and Open Sites) Order 1984 (SI 1984/1992) and the Control of Noise (Code of Practice for Construction and Open Sites) Order 1987 (SI 1987/1730)). The local authority is also required to take into account the need to secure that the best practicable means are employed to minimise noise (s 71(4)).

Service of notice

A notice is served on the person who appears to the local authority to be carrying out or about to carry out the works and other persons responsible for or having control over or carrying out the works. An appeal is available to the magistrates' court within 21 days of the service of the notice but, subject to that, failure to comply with the notice results in an offence.

Prior consent for work on construction sites

It is open to any person operating a construction site to take pro-active steps to secure a local authority consent and this is dealt with under COPA 1974, section 61. By section 61(3) an application is required to contain particulars of the works, the method by which they are to be carried out and the steps proposed to be taken to minimise noise resulting from those works. A consent in response to the notice (for which no form is prescribed) may be issued by the local authority either with or without conditions and a timetable. The effect of the consent is to avoid any action which the local authority may take under section 60, but it should be noted that it does not exempt the successful applicant from the consequences of section 59 (summary proceedings by occupier of premises). A refusal of consent may be the subject of an appeal to the magistrates' court (s 60(7)).

Noise abatement zones

Continuing the theme of pro-activity by local authorities in regard to noise, section 63 of COPA 1974 provides for the designation by a local authority of all or any part of its area as a noise abatement zone. The procedure for doing this is set out in Schedule 1 to the Act but it has been revised by Schedule 2 to the Local Government Planning and Land Act 1980.

Consequence of noise abatement zone – noise level registers

Once the noise abatement order is made, it triggers responsibilities on the local authority to take steps, as soon as practicable, to record the level of noise emanating from premises of a class prescribed in the order. All measurements will need to be recorded in a noise level register with copies of entries served on relevant owners and occupiers. Such owners and occupiers may appeal to the Secretary of State against the record within 28 days if they wish to object to its accuracy. This is often important because otherwise the validity or accuracy of any entry in the register is not to be questioned in any proceedings under this part of the Act. The register is open to public inspection.

Effect of registration

The effect of registration is that the recorded level of noise may not be exceeded except with consent of the local authority. Applications for consent are dealt with under section 65 of COPA 1974.

Reduction of noise levels

A second consequence of the establishment of a noise abatement zone is that it is open to the local authority to take steps to reduce noise deriving from any premises. It will do this under section 66 of COPA 1974 by serving a notice on the person responsible requiring reduction in the level of noise, the prevention of any subsequent increase without consent and the taking of such steps as specified in the notice to achieve these purposes. The notice is known by the terms of the section as a "noise reduction notice" which will set a time-limit being not less than six months from the date of the service of the notice within which the noise level is to be reduced. Particulars of the noise reduction notice must be recorded in the noise level register (see above). There is a right of appeal against the noise reduction notice to the magistrates' court within three months of the date of service.

Practitioners should give consideration to the Control of Noise (Measurement and Registers) Regulations 1976 (SI 1976/37).

Appeals

It will have been noted that there are various rights of appeal deriving from provisions in COPA 1974. The procedure for dealing with appeals is set out in the Control of Noise (Appeals) Regulations 1975 (SI 1975/2116).

Operation of loudspeakers in streets or roads and audible intruder alarms

The Noise and Statutory Nuisance Act 1993 came into force on 5 January 1994. In relation to noise the relevant local authority may adopt the powers granted by sections 8 and 9. The effect of a resolution in relation to section 8 is to bring into force Schedule 2 to the Act, which requires certain consents to be granted on application for the operation of a loudspeaker where it would otherwise be in contravention of section 62 of COPA 1974 (control of noise in streets).

The local authority may also adopt section 9 of the 1993 Act which brings into force, for their area, Schedule 3, relating to audible intruder alarms. This imposes standards and procedures for premises where such alarms are installed. It also allows an officer of the local authority to have access to any premises where an audible alarm gives reasonable cause for annoyance to persons living or working in the vicinity.

Part 2

Applications for Approvals and Other Procedures

Contents of Chapter 6

Chapter 6
Statutory Nuisances

Introduction

Hitherto in this book the statutory codes have been dealt with by reference to separate aspects of the environment. However, the most commonly encountered procedures transcend those boundaries and, as we shall see, cover a whole range of different environmental offences. The law relating to statutory nuisance is now embodied in the Environmental Protection Act 1990 (EPA 1990), Part III. This offers to the local public health authority a procedure for dealing with nuisance if it is satisfied that the statutory nuisance exists or is likely to occur or recur. In brief, the action to be taken includes the service of an abatement notice, in respect of which the person served may appeal to the magistrates' court within 21 days. The court has power to support, modify or dismiss the abatement notice. If the notice is confirmed, failure to comply with it is an offence and at this stage the local public health authority may itself take the necessary action and recover its costs. Additionally, failure to comply with an abatement notice can result in liability on summary conviction to a fine not exceeding £20,000.

The provisions of EPA 1990, sections 79 to 85 came into force on 1 January 1991. Some amendments to the statutory nuisance provisions have been made by the Noise and Statutory Nuisance Act 1993 (see below and Chapter 5). There are regulations relating to appeals (*i.e.* the Statutory Nuisance (Appeals) Regulations 1990 (SI 1990/2276). Notices served under the now repealed Control of Pollution Act 1974 may, nonetheless, be preserved (see *Aitkin* v *South Hams District Council* (1994) *The Times*, 8 July).

What is a statutory nuisance?

In general terms "statutory nuisance" is defined by section 79 of EPA 1990 as:

(i) any premises in such a state as to be prejudicial to health or a nuisance;

(ii) smoke emitted from premises so as to be prejudicial to health or a nuisance;

(iii) fumes or gas emitted from premises so as to be prejudicial to health or a nuisance;

(iv) any dust, steam, smell or other effluvia arising on industrial, trade or business premises and being prejudicial to health or a nuisance;

(v) any accumulation or deposit which is prejudicial to health or a nuisance;

(vi) any animal kept in such a place or manner as to be prejudicial to health or a nuisance;

(vii) noise emitted from premises so as to be prejudicial to health or a nuisance; and

(viii) any other matter declared by any enactment to be a statutory nuisance.

The Noise and Statutory Nuisance Act 1993 has amended EPA 1990 so that a further category of statutory nuisance, noise that is prejudicial to health or a nuisance and is emitted from or caused by vehicle machinery or equipment in a street, has been added. "Equipment" includes a musical instrument.

There have been a large number of cases in which the definition of "statutory nuisance" has been considered, of which the following may be noted: *Pontardawe RDC v Moore-Gwyn* [1929] 1 Ch 656 (premises); *National Coal Board v Thorn* [1976] 1 WLR 543 (nuisance); *Coventry City Council v Cartwright* [1975] 1 WLR 845 (prejudicial to health); *Malton Board of Health v Malton Manure Co* [1879] 4 Ex D 302 (effluvia); *Wivenhoe Port v Colchester Borough Council* [1985] JPL 175 (dust); *R v Walden-Jones ex parte Coton* [1963] Crim LR 839 (animals); *Galer v Morrissey* [1955] 1 A11 ER 380 (noisy animal); *Tower Hamlets LBC v Manzoni and Walder* [1984] 148 JP 123 (noise); and *Southwark LBC v Ince* [1989] 21 HLR 504 (noise).

Summary proceedings

The action to be taken by the local authority where they believe that a statutory nuisance arises or might occur or recur is to serve an abatement notice which can require the nuisance to be stopped or reduced or which can seek the prevention of its occurrence or recurrence. The notice may also require the execution of works and the taking of other steps to achieve these purposes. The notice is required to set time-limits for the taking of any necessary action. It is usually to be served on the person responsible for the nuisance but, where that person cannot be found, the notice goes to the owner or occupier of the premises. In cases where the complaint is of a defect of structural character, the owner of the premises in question must receive the notice. In the case of a statutory nuisance involving noise in a street which has either not yet occurred or arises from an unattended vehicle, machinery or equipment, slightly different service requirements are imposed. In these cases the notice is served on the person responsible for the vehicle, machinery or equipment if that person can be found. Otherwise the notice is permitted to be fixed to the relevant vehicle, machinery or equipment (s 80A).

Certain proceedings may not be started by the local authority without the consent of the Secretary of State, where smoke, fumes, gas, dust, steam, smell or other effluvia emitted from premises are the subject of Part I of EPA 1990. These matters are the responsibility of HM Inspectorate of Pollution. The intention is to avoid duplication of controls.

A special defence is available in cases of abatement notices served in respect of industry, trade or business premises where the nuisance relates to (i), (iv), (v), (vi) and (vii) in the definitions of statutory nuisance (above). The defence is also available in respect of (ii) but not where the nuisance constitutes smoke emitted from a chimney. This is known as the "best practicable means" defence (see below).

Appeals

By section 80 of EPA 1990 anyone receiving a notice may appeal to the magistrates' court within 21 days of the date on which he was served with the notice. If he does not do this and does not comply with the notice, he is liable to prosecution.

Rights to appeal are established by section 80(3) and the procedures for this are set out in the Statutory Nuisance (Appeals) Regulations 1990 (SI 1990/2276). There is a substantial list of grounds of appeal of which the following is a summary.

(i)   The abatement notice is not justified by section 80 of EPA 1990.

(ii) There has been some informality, defect or error in the notice.

(iii) The authority has refused unreasonably to accept compliance with alternative requirements or the requirements of the abatement notice are otherwise unreasonable in character or extent, or are unnecessary.

(iv) The time given by the abatement notice for compliance is not reasonably sufficient.

(v) The best practicable means (see below) have been used to prevent or counteract the effects of the nuisance – only available in respect of the nuisances mentioned above and (so far as appeals are concerned) in relation to smoke emitted from a chimney.

(vi) In the case of a nuisance relating to noise, that the requirements are more onerous than those in force as a result of notices relating to the control of noise levels, served under sections 60 to 67 of the Control of Pollution Act 1974 (see Chapter 5).

(vii) That the abatement notice should or might have been served on some other person, besides or in addition to the appellant. In most cases under this ground the appellant is required to serve a copy of his notice of appeal on that other person.

Appeal hearing

The magistrates' court is required either to quash the abatement notice, vary it if this can be done in favour of the appellant or dismiss it. During the period of the appeal the abatement notice is suspended, except in the special case where it alleges injury to health or that the nuisance is or is anticipated to be of limited duration.

Complaint by a member of the public

Whilst normally the aggrieved member of the public would complain about a nuisance to the public health authority who could be expected to take the appropriate action, an alternative option is to make use of section 82 of the EPA 1990. This entitles a member of the public to make a complaint direct to the magistrates' court on the ground that he is aggrieved by the existence of a statutory nuisance. Upon being satisfied as to this, the court is required to make an order on the defendant to abate the nuisance, to prohibit recurrence and to execute any necessary works. The power to fine the defendant is also available. It is to be noted that the "best practicable means" defence is also available here. Penalties are specified in section 80(5) and (6).

"Best practicable means"

The defence of "best practicable means" has its roots in the Public Health Act 1936 and acknowledges the need for reasonableness in applying the requirements of the law of nuisance in the case of business premises and activities where compliance might well result in an uneconomic operation. Reduced to its basics, the concept takes account of the jobs versus environment argument.

The term "best practicable means" is interpreted in section 79(9) of EPA 1990 as follows:

(a) "Practicable" means reasonably practicable having regard among other things to local conditions and circumstances, to the current state of technical knowledge and to the financial implications.
(b) The means to be employed include the design, installation, maintenance and manner and periods of operation of plant and machinery, and the design, construction and maintenance of buildings and structures.
(c) The test is to apply only so far as compatible with any duty imposed by law.
(d) The test is to apply only so far as compatible with safety and safe working conditions and with the exigencies of any emergency or unforeseeable circumstances.

Some guidance in the interpretation of the definition in relation to noise can be found in codes of practice which have been published under section 71 of the Control of Pollution Act 1974.

It is important to appreciate that the best practicable means defence is by no means a soft option for industry. See, for example, *Scholefield* v *Schunck* [1855] 19 JP 84 and *Wivenhoe Port* v *Colchester Borough Council* [1985] JPL 175.

Recovery of expenses

Any expenses reasonably incurred by a local authority in abating or preventing the recurrence of a statutory nuisance where an abatement notice has been served and not complied with may be recovered, if necessary through the court, from the person responsible for the nuisance or from the owner (EPA 1990, s 80(4)). Furthermore, since 5 January 1993 a new section 81A has been inserted into the Act by the Noise and Statutory Nuisance Act 1993. This provides that any recoverable expenses may be a charge on the premises in question.

Contents of Chapter 7

Chapter 7
Water

Abstraction

Water Resources Act 1991

There are a limited number of people who may apply for a licence to abstract water. Occupation of the land adjacent to the inland water or above the underground strata is usually required.

Inland water

Inland waters are defined by section 221 of the Water Resources Act 1991 (WRA 1991) and, in general, will include a river, stream or other watercourse either natural, artificial or tidal. They will also include any lake or pond, reservoir or dock. The resources, in each case, may be natural or artificial. Also included in the definition is so much of any channel, creek, bay, estuary or arm of the sea which lies within the National Rivers Authority (NRA) area. The regional office of the NRA will be in a position to define this. A person who wishes to abstract from an inland water must be the occupier of land contiguous to it or (when the licence is granted) have a right of access to that land.

Underground strata

Underground strata is defined by section 221 of WRA 1991 to mean largely what it says. The person entitled to abstract from underground strata is the occupier of the land where the underground strata is or, where there is an excavation into underground strata, the person who, when the licence has effect, has a right of access to the land above the underground strata.

Applications for licences to abstract

The procedure for applications is dealt with in the Water Resources (Licences) Regulations 1965 (SI 1965/534). Model forms of application are set out in Schedule 1 to the Regulations. An application is made to the NRA on the form which is obtainable from them. The application is required to be accompanied by a map to a scale of not less that six inches to one mile or the metric equivalent. The map must show every point of abstraction proposed and the land which is occupied by the applicant. In most cases the application must also show the land on which it is proposed to use the water. In circumstances where the water is to be used for different purposes, this should be distinguished on the map. Where the applicant is not the occupier, evidence must be provided which will show that access to the relevant land will be available if the licence is granted.

Notice under section 37

Section 37 of WRA 1991 requires publication of notice in the *London Gazette* of an application for a licence and at least once in each of two successive weeks in local newspapers. If the licence is for abstraction from an inland water the notice must, not later than the date on which it was first published in the local newspaper, be served on any navigation authority, harbour authority or conservancy authority responsible for that inland water at the point of proposed abstraction. The internal drainage board must also be served as must any local water undertaker.

Contents of the newspaper notice

Forms of the notice are set out in Schedule 2 to the 1965 Regulations (see above). Besides describing the proposals, the notices are required by section 37 of WRA 1991 to name a place in the locality where a copy of the application and other submitted documents can be inspected at all reasonable hours and state that any person may make representations in writing to the NRA concerning the application before the end of the period specified in the notice (*i.e.* not less than 28 days from the date of local advertisement).

Documents required

The applicant must send to the NRA the forms of application and plans, copies of the newspapers containing the appropriate section 37 notice and a declaration signed on behalf of the applicant that the notice has been published in the *London Gazette* (giving the date of publication). Where the notice has been served on any authority, details must be given in the declaration.

Application for a licence to impound or for a combined licence

Impounding of an inland water is forbidden unless a licence is granted by the NRA and other conditions contained in section 37 of WRA 1991 are met.

Procedure for application

The procedure is controlled by regulation 8 of the 1965 Regulations (see above) and is similar to that for an abstraction licence. A map must accompany the application showing, *inter alia*, the location of the impounding works, the extent of such land to be submerged and any points of discharge.

Newspaper advertisements and notice to other authorities are required in the same way as for a licence to abstract (see above).

There are also special provisions in regulation 8 for a combined abstraction/impounding licence.

Succession to a licence

Succession to a licence is dealt with under sections 49 and 50 of WRA 1991 and is mainly a formal matter of notification to the NRA.

Revocation or variation of licence

(i) On Application By Holder

This is a simple application under section 51 of WRA 1991 and regulation 9 of the 1965 Regulations. In the case of variation, the procedures for publicity will also apply in the same way as for the licence applications (see above), unless the variation is limited simply to reducing the quantity of water authorised to be abstracted.

(ii) By The National Rivers Authority

If the NRA decides to revoke or vary a licence it is obliged to notify the holder and give publicity similar to that mentioned above. The holder has a right to object (s 53(4)) at which stage the proposals are referred to the Secretary of State who will make the decision. However, if no objection is raised the matter may be dealt with by the NRA. In the circumstances defined by section 61, compensation for revocation or variation will follow.

Application period

The NRA has three months to consider applications for licences or variations. In default of a decision within that period or such extended period as is agreed with him, the applicant may appeal to the Secretary of State on grounds of non-determination.

Appeals

An appeal against a decision of the NRA or in default of decision may be made to the Secretary of State. There is no specified form but the appeal is required to be in writing and a copy must be served on the NRA. All this must be undertaken within 28 days from the date when any decision was notified to the appellant (WRA 1991, s 43).

The procedure for appeals is governed by regulation 12 of the 1965 Regulations.

Water pollution

Water Industry Act 1991

There is a right subject to the consent of the water company for the area and to the provisions of the Water Industry Act 1991 (WIA 1991) to discharge trade effluents into public sewers. A "trade effluent" is defined by section 141 to mean any liquid, either with or without particles of matter in suspension in the liquid which is wholly or partly produced in the course of any trade or industry carried on at trade premises and, in relation to any trade premises, means any such liquid which is so produced in the course of any trade or industry carried on at those premises, but does not include domestic sewage.

"Trade premises" means any premises used or intended to be used for carrying on any trade or industry, including farms, smallholdings and the like, and laboratories.

Procedure

Trade effluent may not be discharged from any trade premises except in accordance with a written application. This is served on the appropriate water company for the area. There is no prescribed form but section 119 of WIA 1991 specifies that the application must contain details of the nature or composition of the trade effluent, the maximum quantity of the effluent proposed to be discharged per day and the highest rate at which discharge will take place. The application is required to be served by the owner or occupier of the premises in question,

It is open to the appropriate water company for the area to prohibit the discharge or issue a consent with or without specific conditions. The extent to which conditions may be imposed is defined in section 121.

Sometimes, the application for consent relates to what is known as special category effluent, generally containing especially polluting substances. The term is defined in section 141 and is prescribed by the Secretary of State under the Trade Effluents (Prescribed Processes and Substances) Regulations 1989 (SI 1989/ 1156). These applications are required to be referred to the Secretary of State under the procedures set out in section 120.

Appeals

Where an owner or occupier is refused a consent or is dissatisfied with the condition of that consent, he may avail himself of the right of appeal under section 122 of WIA 1991. He may also appeal if the water company has failed to deal with the matter within a two-month period. The appeal is made to the Director General of Water Services who has power to give the necessary consent, with or without condition. The right of appeal is also available in regard to the discharge of special category effluent (s 123).

Trade effluent agreements

Section 129 of WIA 1991 provides for agreements to be made with the appropriate water company for the area. The agreement can relate to the reception and disposal by the water company of any trade effluent produced on the owner/occupier's premises and can deal with the construction by the water company of any works required for reception or disposal and payment of expenses by the owner/occupier.

Agreements made under section 7 of the Public Health (Drainage of Trade Premises) Act 1937 are preserved, on the repeal of that Act, by Schedule 8 to WIA 1991.

Powers to vary conditions

The water company has the power to vary conditions of any previously consented discharge of trade effluent into a public sewer. These powers arise from sections 124 to 128 of WIA 1991.

Extension of WIA 1991 to other effluents

Section 139 of WIA 1991 gives power to the Secretary of State for the Environment to extend the definition of trade effluents to other types of effluent. The orders are sometimes local in nature and practitioners would need to confirm with the local water company whether such orders apply in the area in question.

Authority for discharges

A person avoids an offence under section 85 of WRA 1991 by securing and complying with either a consent under that Act or the Control of Pollution Act 1974 or a licence granted under Part II of the Food and Environment Protection Act 1985 (discharge of substances into the sea) or an authorisation for a prescribed process designated for central control granted under Part I of the Environmental Protection Act 1990 (integrated pollution control authorisation) or any local Act or prescribed enactment. A discharge in accordance with section 163 of WRA 1991 or section 165 of WIA 1991 (discharges for works' purposes) will, generally, also avoid an offence. It is to be noted that WRA 1991 also controls discharges to "controlled waters", defined in section 104 of the Act. The definition is a long one but, in general terms, includes the sea, rivers and watercourses, lakes and ponds, the underground aquifer and underground excavations.

Applications for consent

Applications for consent are made under section 88 of, and Schedule 10 to WRA 1991. The procedures of Schedule 10 require an application to be made to the NRA, who itself must publish notice of the application in local newspapers and in the *London Gazette*. A copy of the application is required to be sent by the NRA to every local authority or water undertaker where the discharge is to occur, and, where such discharge is into coastal waters, copies must also be served on the Secretary of State and the Minister of Agriculture, Fisheries and Food. Publicity for the application may be avoided in circumstances where the authority proposes to give the consent applied for and considers the discharge will have "no appreciable effect" on the receiving waters. The phrase has been considered in relation to the Control of Pollution Act 1974 by Department of the Environment Circular 17/84, "Water and the Environment".

Contents of Chapter 8

Chapter 8
Industrial Air Pollution and Integrated Pollution Control

Control of Industrial Air Pollution (Registration of Works) Regulations 1989

At the time of writing, the Control of Industrial Air Pollution (Regulation of Works) Regulations 1989 (SI 1989/318) represent one of the two systems for control of air pollution by major processes. The Regulations envisage a requirement for application for registration. However, the requirement for registration has now largely been overtaken by the obligation imposed by Part I of the Environmental Protection Act 1990 (see Chapter 2 and p 103 below). The present programme envisages that the 1989 Regulations will become obsolete by the end of January 1996, on which date all processes prescribed under the 1990 Act will be the subject of that Act. This registration is required to be made by the owner of the works in question, who must supply the following particulars:

(i) the name and address of the owner of the works and, if the company is registered under the Companies Act 1989, the name, registered number and registered office of the company;

(ii) the name and address of the premises where the works is situated;

(iii) the identification of the works by reference to a map or plan or otherwise;

(iv) the name of the relevant local authority;

(v) the date on which the application is made;

(vi) a full description of the nature of the work carried on or proposed to be carried on;

(vii) a description of the source, nature and amount of any noxious or offensive substance that may be emitted into the atmosphere as a result of carrying on the works;

(viii) a description of the means proposed to enable the works to be carried on in accordance with the legislation;

(ix) a description of the provision which the applicant has proposed to make for determining the nature and amount of any noxious or offensive substance emitted into the atmosphere (monitoring).

Notice of application

The application is made to the Secretary of State for the Environment, although administration is devolved to Her Majesty's Inspectorate of Pollution (HMIP). There is a requirement by regulation 4 of the 1989 Regulations to publish, within 14 days of the application in a local newspaper and in successive weeks, a notice giving details of the application, an indication of the place where the application may be inspected and a statement to the effect that written representations can be made to the Secretary of State within 21 days of the first newspaper publication. A copy of the notice is required to be sent to the Secretary of State, together with the certificate of publication. The combined effect of regulations 4 and 5 is that the notice of application must be advertised between 14 days and six months after the date on which the application has been received by the Secretary of State.

Public access to applications

Whilst, in the main, all applications are available for inspection by the public, there are provisions for the Secretary of State to exempt from disclosure any particulars which would prejudice unreasonably some private interest concerning a trade secret or prejudice the interests of national defence. The local authority also has obligations to keep the application available for inspection.

The register

All works required to be registered must be recorded in a register for that purpose as controlled by regulation 7 of the 1989 Regulations, to which the public has access. A duplicate part of the register relating to works within its area is also made available by the Secretary of State to the local authority in question.

Certificate of registration

The certificate of registration confirms that the works are registered for the purposes of the legislation and remains in force until the work to which it relates is closed for a period of 12 months or more or a new certificate is issued in replacement (reg 9).

Notification of changes to works

The owner must notify changes appropriate to the certificate of registration within one month of the change taking place.

Integrated pollution and air pollution control by local authorities

Regulations under the Environmental Protection Act 1990

Part I of the Environmental Protection Act 1990 (EPA 1990) will be brought into force for all new prescribed processes. This began in 1991 and is expected to be concluded by January 1996.

There are now a number of sets of regulations which control procedures and applications for authorisations under the integrated pollution control provisions of the Act. The regulations also deal with applications to local public health authorities for authorisations for those lesser polluting processes and, here, the control is limited to air pollution only (although other controls may apply by virtue of other legislation).

Prescribed processes and substances

It is first necessary to clarify whether a given process is the subject of integrated pollution control (IPC) or local authority control. This may be ascertained by reference to the Environmental Protection (Prescribed Processes and Substances) Regulations 1991 (SI 1991/472). These Regulations, which came into force in England and Wales on 1 April 1991, set out, in Schedule 1, descriptions of the various processes in respect of which authorisations are required. The Schedule divides processes into part A and part B. Part A lists processes the subject of IPC, whilst part B describes processes which will be controlled by local authorities. See Appendices A and B (at pp 147 and 149) for general lists respectively of these processes. The main Regulations have been amended on a number of occasions by the Environmental Protection (Amendment of Regulations) Regulations 1991 (SI 1991/836), the Environmental Protection (Prescribed Processes and Substances) (Amendment) Regulations 1992 (SI 1992/614) and similarly named amendment regulations numbered SI 1993/1749, SI 1993/2405, SI 1994/1271 and SI 1994/1329.

Once it is concluded that the process is caught by the Regulations, attention needs to be paid to the rules relating to applications.

Applications, appeals and registers

Applications, appeals and registers are controlled by the Environmental Protection (Applications, Appeals and Registers) Regulations 1991 (SI 1991/507). These Regulations deal in detail with the procedures to be followed where it is necessary to make applications for authorisation to carry on a prescribed process. It should be noted that in the initial years of EPA 1990, an application for an authorisation will be needed only where (i) there is a new process, (ii) an existing process is substantially changed and (iii) where further regulations provide that specific processes, whether new or existing, require a specific authorisation.

The above Regulations set out in detail what is required. See Appendix D (at p 155) for a typical application form.

Guidance notes

A wide range of guidance notes have been prepared and these fall into four categories.

(i)   General – examples are "Integrated Pollution Control. A Practical Guide" (published by the Department of the Environment and the Welsh Office), general guidance notes for local authorities (GG1–5) (published by the Department of the Environment, the Scottish Office and Welsh Office).

(ii) Industry sector guides IPR 1–5 covering the main industrial sectors and giving general guidance on the processes and procedures.

(iii) Specific industry guidance notes, which relate to particular processes and the substances produced by the processes which are under the control of EPA 1990.

(iv) Updating guidance notes (U–G series).

Determination periods

The Secretary of State has also published the Environmental Protection (Authorisation of Processes) (Determination Periods) Order 1991 (SI 1991/513), which set down time-limits for consideration of authorisation applications. The Regulations are, in essence, variations of the period set out in Schedule 1 to EPA 1990 (usually four months), although by sections 21 and 22 there are special arrangements in the circumstances where confidentiality of parts of the applications is sought.

The timetable for implementing IPC (during a period extending to the end of 1995) is set out in Appendix A to the integrated pollution control practical guide (referred to in (i) above).

Contents of Chapter 9

Chapter 9
Waste on Land

Applications under the Control of Pollution Act 1974

Introduction

Before 1 May 1994, applications for licences to dispose of waste were controlled by section 5 of the Control of Pollution Act 1974 (COPA 1974). The procedure was governed by the Collection and Disposal of Waste Regulations 1988 (SI 1988/819). By section 5(2) a disposal authority could not issue a licence until it was satisfied that planning consent under the Town and Country Planning Act 1990 was in force for the use of the land, plant or equipment to which the licence was to relate. Once that consent was in force the waste disposal authority could not reject the application unless it was satisfied that its rejection was necessary for the prevention of pollution of water or danger to public health.

By section 5(4) a disposal authority proposing to issue a licence had to consult, before it did so:

(i) the National Rivers Authority (NRA);
(ii) in the case of the London Waste Regulation Authority, any London waste disposal authority and any collection authority whose area included any part of the relevant land;
(iii) in all other cases, any collection authority in whose area the land in question was included.

The disposal authority's responsibility also included the duty to consider any representation received from the above-mentioned bodies within 21 days (or a longer period if agreed between them). In circumstances where the NRA requested the disposal authority not to issue the licence or disagreed with proposed conditions of the licence, then either body could refer the matter to the Secretary of State. The licence was not issued except in accordance with his decision.

Conditions of a licence

Section 6 of COPA 1974 made provision for the conditions of any disposal licence. These conditions related to:

(i)   the duration of the licence;

(ii)   the supervision by the holder of activities to which the licence related;

(iii)   the kinds and qualities of waste which could be dealt with in pursuance of the licence, the methods of dealing with them and the recording of information;

(iv)   precautions to be taken on the land to which the licence related;

(v)   the steps to be taken to facilitate compliance with conditions of the planning permission on which the licence was based;

(vi)   the hours of working;

(vii)   any works to be carried out in connection with the land, plant or equipment to which the licence related, before the activities authorised by the licence were begun or while they were continuing.

Appeal against non-determination

An applicant could appeal against non-determination after two months had elapsed from the date when the disposal authority received the application or such longer period as the authority and the applicant agreed in writing.

Variation of conditions and revocation of licences

Variation of conditions of an extant licence could be pursued in two alternative ways:

(i)   by the disposal authority – the authority could serve a notice on the holder of the licence modifying the conditions specified to any extent, which in the opinion of the authority, was desirable and which was unlikely to require unreasonable expenditure by the licence holder;

(ii) by the licence holder – the licence holder could request a modification, secured by notice from the disposal authority confirming the modification.

Section 7 of COPA 1974 imposed an obligation on the disposal authority to make a modification of a licence in circumstances where pollution of water or danger to public health could arise or where there could be serious detriment to the amenities of the locality affected by the activities the subject of the licence. However, by section 7(4) if the danger of pollution of water or to public health or to local amenity was so serious that a modification of a condition was inadequate, then the duty of the authority was to revoke the licence.

Transfer and relinquishment of licences

The holder of a disposal licence could transfer such licence by giving notice to the authority indicating the date of transfer and details of the name and address of the transferee. The disposal authority had the right, within eight weeks of the notice having been received, to give counter-notice to the transferee that it declined to accept him as holder of the licence. Thereupon the licence ceased to have effect after a further period of two weeks.

Section 8(4) of COPA 1974 enabled the holder of a disposal licence to cancel it by simple delivery to the authority which issued it and notice to that authority that he no longer required the licence. However, it should be noted that this right was brought to an end when Part II of the Environmental Protection Act 1990 was brought into force on 1 May 1994.

All these provisions of COPA 1974 are, therefore, replaced (see below).

Applications under the Environmental Protection Act 1990

The Environmental Protection Act 1990 (EPA 1990) contains new powers in relation to waste management licences. These powers are contained in sections 35 to 44 and replace the provisions relating to waste disposal licences contained in COPA 1974. The powers under EPA 1990 relating to applications were brought into force, with effect from 1 May 1994, by the Environmental Protection Act 1990 (Commencement No 15) Order 1994 (SI 1994/1096).

Waste management licences

A waste management licence is granted by the waste regulation authority and will authorise the treatment, keeping or disposal of controlled waste in or on specified land or the treatment or disposal by means of a specified mobile plant.

The considerations to be taken into account by the waste regulation authority on receipt of an application for a licence under Part II of EPA 1990 have been greatly extended. Considerable further detail is available in DoE Circular 11/94, "Environmental Protection Act 1990: Part II: Waste Management Licensing: The Framework Directive on Waste" and Waste Management Paper No 4, "Licensing of Waste Management Facilities".

Application

An application is required to be made by:

(i) the occupier in the case of a licence relating to the treatment, keeping or disposal of waste in or on land;

(ii) the operator in the case of a licence for the treatment or disposal of waste by means of a mobile plant.

The application is to be made on a form, usually issued by the waste regulation authority and will be made to the authority where the land is situated (Waste Management Licensing Regulations 1994 (SI 1994/1056), reg 2). However, in the case of a mobile plant licence the operator must apply to the authority where he has his principal place of business. A fee for the application is prescribed and will be payable under section 41. The required information is specified in Schedule 2 to the 1994 Regulations. Fees are set out in the Waste Management Licensing (Fees and Charges) Scheme 1994.

No licence may be issued unless planning permission is in force or a certificate establishing the use for the purpose exists under the Town and Country Planning Act 1990.

The waste regulation authority may not reject a properly made application unless:

(i) the applicant is not a fit and proper person (see below);
(ii) rejection is necessary for the purpose of preventing pollution of the environment, harm to human health or serious detriment to the amenities of the locality.

However, the last justification for refusal of an application (relating to amenity) is inapplicable where planning permission is in force in relation to the use which will be the subject of the licence.

Consultations

The waste regulation authority may not issue a licence until it has referred the proposal to the NRA and the Health and Safety Executive and considered any representations made by those bodies within the allowed period of 21 days starting from the day when the proposal is received by the waste disposal authority. However, section 35(10) of EPA 1990 allows the authorities, apparently without reference to the applicant, to agree a longer period. The applicant's sanction is to appeal on non-determination grounds (see below).

National Rivers Authority

In the cases where a proposal has been referred to the NRA, who request that the licence not be issued or who disagree about the conditions of the proposed licence, there is a provision in section 36(5) of EPA 1990 for the matter to be referred to the Secretary of State. Pending his decision by way of arbitration the licence cannot be issued, and may only be issued subsequently in accordance with his decision.

Protection of ground water

Regulation 14 of the 1994 Regulations (see above) provides that where a licence authorises the regeneration of waste oil, conditions must be imposed to avoid certain toxic or dangerous waste. Regulation 14 also forbids the keeping of waste oil where a mixture with any of the above waste would otherwise take place. Regulation 14 implements the requirements of the EC Directive on Waste Oils (75/439/EEC), as amended by Directive 87/101/EEC. Further guidance is provided in DoE Circular 11/94, annex 4, paragraph 4.29.

Further provisions for the protection of ground water are also included in regulation 15 of the 1994 Regulations. This incorporates requirements of the EC Directive on the Protection of Ground Water against Pollution caused by Certain Dangerous Substances (80/68/EEC). For further information see DoE Circulars 4/82, 20/90 and Circular 11/94, annex 7.

Conditions of a licence

By section 35(3) of EPA 1990 a licence is required to be granted on such terms and conditions as appear to the waste regulation authority to be appropriate. They may relate to the activities which the licence authorises and to the precautions to be taken and works to be carried out in connection with or in consequence of the activities. Conditions may require the licence-holder to carry out works or do other things even though he is not entitled to do so. Section 35(4) appears to contain an entirely novel provision to the effect that any person whose consent would be required *shall* grant or join in granting the holder of the licence such rights in relation to the land as will enable the holder of the licence to comply with any requirements imposed on him by the licence.

Besides fees for applications for licences there will be an annual "subsistence" charge, designed ultimately to cover the costs of monitoring licenced sites. This may include an additional charge for the NRA if they had been consulted in the prior year. Subsistence charges are payable by 30 April in each year, otherwise the licensee risks revocation for non-payment, against which there is no appeal.

The Secretary of State has provided detailed guidance on conditions to be included in a licence either directly or by reference to submitted working plans (see Waste Management Paper WMP4, "The Licensing of Waste Disposal Sites", 3rd ed (1994)).

Surrender and transfer

The EPA 1990 makes changes in relation to surrender and transfer which may not be secured except in the special circumstances of sections 39 and 40 (below).

Variation

A licence may be varied under section 37:

(i) on the waste regulation authority's initiative. A condition of a licence may be modified as may be considered desirable by the authority, provided that the condition is unlikely to require unreasonable expense on the part of the holder; and

(ii) on the initiative of the licence-holder. The conditions may be modified to the extent requested in the application but at the discretion of the authority. A fee is payable under section 41.

Modification

The waste regulation authority has further responsibilities under section 37(2) to modify the conditions of a licence where this is required for the purpose of ensuring that the activities authorised do not cause pollution of the environment or harm to human health or become seriously detrimental to the amenities of the locality affected by the activities.

The process of modification is secured by notice served on the holder of the licence and it must state the time when the modification is to take effect.

Decisions on variation and modification frequently require the waste regulation authority to balance environmental and economic factors. The Waste Management Paper series published by the Secretary of State gives guidance in this area. See, for example, WMP4, "The Licensing of Waste Disposal Sites" 3rd ed (1994), WMP26, "Landfilling Wastes – A Technical Memorandum for the Disposal of Wastes on Landfill Sites" (1986), and WMP27, "Landfill Gas – A Technical Memorandum on the Monitoring and Control of Landfill", 2nd ed (1991).

Revocation and suspension of licences

Under section 38 of EPA 1990 revocation and suspension of a licence may be undertaken by the waste regulation authority where:

(i) the holder has ceased to be a fit and proper person by reason of a conviction for a relevant offence (Waste Management Licensing Regulations 1994 (SI 1994/1056), reg 3);

(ii) that the continuation of the licenced activities would cause pollution of the environment, harm to human health or serious detriment to the amenities of the locality affected;

(iii) that the pollution, harm or detriment cannot be avoided by modification.

Additionally, revocation to the extent specified may be exercised by the waste regulation authority where the holder has ceased to be a fit and proper person by reason of the management of the activities authorised by the licence having ceased to be in the hands of a technically competent person. (For "fit and proper person" see p 120 below.)

EFFECT OF REVOCATION

Once a licence is revoked in part it will cease to have effect to authorise the carrying on of the activities specified, but it is open to the authority to retain further requirements imposed by the licence which the authority will require should continue to bind the licence-holder. This might arise where the right to continue to dispose of waste ceases, but the obligation to prevent pollution caused by earlier disposals of waste may be required to continue.

SUSPENSION OF LICENCE

Under section 38 of EPA 1990 a licence can be suspended by a waste regulation authority where:

(i) the holder has ceased to be a fit and proper person (see p 120 below) by reason of the management of the activities authorised by the licence having ceased to be in the hands of a technically competent person; or

(ii) that serious pollution of the environment or serious harm to human health results from or is about to be caused by the activities to which the licence relates or some happening or threatened happening affecting those activities; and

(iii) serious pollution of the environment or serious harm to human health will result if the activities or the circumstances persist.

The effect of suspension is that those activities approved by the licence, or some of them as identified by the authority, are suspended. The suspension notice may require the holder of the licence to take measures to deal with or avert the pollution or harm. Failure to comply is an offence (s 38(10)).

Revocation or suspension is effected by notice served on the holder by the waste regulation authority, which notice is required to state the time when any requirement is to take effect. The notice may also specify when the suspension is to cease and in what circumstances.

Surrender of licence

The EPA 1990 makes significant changes to the powers of a licence-holder to surrender his licence. During the currency of COPA 1974 a surrender could be affected at will and without any need for agreement by any other party.

With effect from the coming into force of section 39 of EPA 1990 neither site licences under COPA 1974 nor waste management licences under EPA 1990 may be surrendered except under a special regime.

WASTE MANAGEMENT LICENCES

The surrender of waste management licences is expected to be controlled by the conditions upon which the licence will be granted.

SITE LICENCES

Site licences under COPA 1974 may only be surrendered if the authority accepts such surrender. The procedure involves the licence-holder's making an application to the authority on the appropriate form giving information and such evidence as the Secretary of State will prescribe by regulations. A fee is payable. Schedule 1 to the Waste Management Licensing Regulations 1994 (SI 1994/1056) identifies standards and criteria to be met by the licence-holder. These deal with matters relating to pollution and health and safety of the site, including the control of gas and leachate, as well as after-care. It seems likely that considerable periods of time will elapse once the completion of the main waste disposal activities are completed, before surrender can be accepted.

Guidance on the proper approach to surrender applications is included in Waste Management Paper WMP4, "Licensing of Waste Management Facilities", 3rd ed (1994), and WMP26A, "Landfill Completion" (1993).

DUTIES OF AN AUTHORITY ON APPLICATION FOR SURRENDER

Under section 39 of EPA 1990, once the authority has received such application it is required to inspect the land and seek any further information or evidence.

Thereafter the authority is required by section 39(5) to decide whether it is likely that there will be any more pollution of the environment or harm to human health. Only when it is satisfied that pollution or harm will not happen may the authority accept surrender. It may only accept surrender after referring the proposal to the NRA and considering any representations. If the NRA requests that the surrender of the licence not be accepted and a dispute with the authority persists, the matter may be referred to the Secretary of State for decision.

CERTIFICATE OF COMPLETION

Once surrender of the licence is accepted, the authority is required to issue to the applicant a certificate of completion stating its satisfaction. Once the certificate is issued, the licence ceases to have effect.

For further guidance see DoE Circular 11/94, annex 4, paragraphs 4.50 to 4.54.

Transfer of licences

New controls on transfers of licences are to be brought into force by section 40 of EPA 1990. The waste regulation authority will have power to ensure that transfer is only to be made to a "fit and proper person" (see p 120).

An application for transfer must be made jointly by the licence-holder and the proposed transferee (EPA 1990, s 40(2) and reg 2 of and Sched 2 to the 1994 Regulations (see above). See also DoE Circular 11/94, annex 4.55 and 4.56).

Appeals

Appeals are made to the Secretary of State by virtue of section 43 of EPA 1990. Appeals lie on decisions (or failures to make decisions) where:

(i)   an application for a licence or modification of conditions is rejected;
(ii)   a licence is granted subject to conditions;
(iii)   the conditions of a licence are modified;
(iv)   a licence is suspended;
(v)   a licence is revoked;
(vi)   an application to surrender a licence is rejected;
(vii)   an application for the transfer of a licence is rejected.

TIME-LIMITS AND NOTICE OF AN APPEAL

An appeal must be lodged within six months of the rejection of the application or other decision complained of, although the Secretary of State may extend the period. Appeal is made on the form supplied by the Planning Inspectorate, Tollgate House, Houlton Street, Bristol, BS2 9DL. See regulation 6 of the Waste Management Licensing Regulations 1994 and annex 10 to DoE Circular 11/94. Guidance on the exercise of this discretion is set out in Waste Management Paper WMP4, paragraphs 3.17 to 3.35 (see above).

The usual procedure will be for the Secretary of State to appoint an inspector (to whom he may delegate the determination). Any party to the appeal may request or the Secretary of State may decide that a hearing should be undertaken. Once the appeal is determined, the authority is required to give effect to that determination.

Pending the determination of an appeal, modification or revocation the decision in question is ineffective. However, this provision does not apply if the notice of modification or revocation includes a statement that in the opinion of the authority it is necessary for the purpose of preventing or, where that is not practicable, minimising pollution of the environment or harm to human health that the modification or revocation should not apply. However, if the Secretary of State or other person determining the appeal decides that the authority has acted unreasonably then the suspension of modification or revocation may be removed pending the final outcome of the appeal. Furthermore, the holder or former holder is then entitled to compensation from the authority for any loss suffered as a result of the unreasonable action of the authority. Compensation is settled by arbitration in the event of continuing dispute.

Meaning of "fit and proper person"

Unless an applicant for a waste disposal licence satisfies the criteria of "a fit and proper person" such licence may not be issued. Furthermore, any fit or proper person who ceases to be so may be required to forfeit the licence. The measurement of "fit and proper person" is by reference to the licensed activities carried on by that person and the fulfilment of the requirements of the licence.

A person is to be treated as not a fit and proper person if:

(i) he or another relevant person (see below) has been convicted of a relevant offence – prescribed by the 1994 Regulations;
(ii) the management of the activities authorised by the licence is not in the hands of a technically competent person;
(iii) the holder or potential holder of the licence has not made or will not make financial provision adequate to discharge the obligations arising from the licence.

It is to be noted that in relation to paragraph (i) above the treating of a convicted person as not fit and proper is at the discretion of the authority.

The criteria for technical competence are laid down in regulation 4 of the 1994 Regulations. Technical competence relates to the management of the facility or facilities (see WMP4, paras 3.56 to 3.67). The tests for financial competence are not subject to statutory guidance but are extensively dealt with in WMP4, paras 3.68 to 3.122.

RELEVANT PERSON

A relevant person for the purposes of paragraph (i) above is to be treated as a person associated with the licence-holder and as having been convicted of a relevant offence if:

(i) any person has been convicted of a relevant offence in the course of his employment by the holder or carrying on business as a partner of the holder;

(ii) a body corporate has been convicted of a relevant offence when the licence-holder was a director, manager, secretary or similar officer of that body;

(iii) where the holder of the licence is a body corporate and a director, manager, secretary or similar officer has been convicted of a relevant offence or was in a similar position in another body when a relevant offence was committed by that body corporate (EPA 1990, s 74).

Contents of Chapter 10

Chapter 10
Hazardous Substances

Food and Environment Protection Act 1985

Lifting of emergency order

The Secretary of State for the Environment and the Minister of Agriculture, Fisheries and Food both have powers to lift emergency orders (see p 63) in any way they consider appropriate and subject to any conditions. The Act has not laid down procedures for applications other than to make provision for them under section 2(1). Since, in the particular circumstances of an emergency, investigating and enforcement officers will have been empowered to take action, to the extent set out in section 3 of the Act, it is clear that an informal and subsequently formal approach of the officers would be the correct course of action.

Pesticides

See Chapter 4 for a general statement of the implications of Part II of the Act as it applies to pesticides.

Control of Pesticides Regulations 1986

The Control of Pesticides Regulations 1986 (SI 1986/1510) provide, *inter alia*, the mechanisms whereby approvals can be granted for the use, supply and storage of pesticides. Approval can be full or provisional under regulation 5.

By regulation 6, consent to the advertisement of pesticides as well as to the sale, supply, storage and use of them may be given, again subject to conditions. The Schedules to the Regulations set out basic conditions – but further ones may be added. Schedule 4 deals specifically with conditions relating to the application of pesticides from an aircraft.

Planning (Hazardous Substances) Act 1990

Consent under the Planning (Hazardous Substances) Act 1990 is dealt with in sections 6 *et seq.* Applications for consent are made to the hazardous substances authority (see Chapter 4). There is an obligation to consult with the Health and Safety Executive.

The procedures for applications for consents are laid down in the Planning (Hazardous Substances) Regulations 1992 (SI 1992/656) which came into force on 1 June 1992. Forms of application are set out in Schedule 2 to the Regulations. Applications, which are similar to those for planning permission, are dealt with in regulation 5, whilst publicity for applications is provided for in regulations 6 and 7. The hazardous substances authority is required to consult with a range of bodies which consider the application (reg 10) and normally has a period of eight weeks within which to reach a decision (reg 11). A procedure for appeals is included in regulation 13. For further information see DoE Circular 11/92, "Planning Controls for Hazardous Substances".

Environmental Protection Act 1990 – Genetically modified organisms

Consents to the importation, acquisition, release or marketing of any genetically modified organisms are required by section 111 of EPA 1990. The section indicates that an application for a consent must contain such information and be made and advertised in such manner as may be prescribed. A fee is charged in accordance with section 113.

Applications are the subject of the Genetically Modified Organisms (Deliberate Release) Regulations 1992 (SI 1992/3280). An application for a consent to release genetically modified organisms is dealt with in regulation 5. The application is made to the Secretary of State and must contain the information prescribed in regulation 6. Applications are required to be advertised in accordance with regulation 8. The application must contain detailed information, in particular dealing with information prescribed in Schedule 1 to the Regulations as appropriate and on data or results from any previous release of the organisms or similar organisms. An assessment of impacts and risks proposed to human health and the environment is also required.

The Secretary of State will normally be required to consult the European Commission under the procedures established by the Deliberate Release Directive 90/990/EEC. The Secretary of State also has various responsibilities including a proper evaluation of the risks. He may not grant a consent without the agreement of the Health and Safety Executive. Regulation 16 deals with duties of the Secretary of State in relation to applications for consent to market genetically modified organisms. An application will attract a fee in accordance with section 113 of EPA 1990 and the Genetically Modified Organisms (Deliberate Releases) Fees and Charges Scheme 1993.

In the case of the contained use of genetically modified organisms, procedures are set out in Part II of the Genetically Modified Organisms (Contained Use) Regulations 1992 (SI 1992/ 3217). Normally, contained use will not require a consent, provided that Part II is complied with. However, there are limited circumstances where notifications and consents are required.

Part 3

Some Notes on Common Law and other Liabilities and Remedies

Contents of Chapter 11

Chapter 11
Access to Environmental Information

Introduction

"The Government believes that the public should have a right of access to information held by Pollution Control Authorities."

This statement of Government policy, appearing as it did in the Environment White Paper, "This Common Inheritance" (Department of the Environment, 1990), comes towards the end of a significant period of change in the aspirations of individual members of the public and special interest groups for information on environmental issues. Successive governments have long held the view that the all-pervading influence of human activity on the environment must be met by ensuring that society as a whole has a satisfactory means of securing balance between development and natural protection. Thus, since the 1960s there has been an acceleration of statutory provision of public rights to information concerning the environment, as a means to this end.

Routes to public access

Rights of access to public information are, in the main, achieved in one of two ways. Most environmental Acts of Parliament or their derivative regulations provide for public registers of information. These are now augmented by the implementation in the United Kingdom of the Directive on Freedom of Access to Information on the Environment (90/313/EEC). This has been achieved by the Environmental Information Regulations 1992 (SI 1992/3240).

Public registers

The extent and range of information held on public registers will depend upon the individual legislative requirements but, typically, a register entry will be likely to hold the following information:

(i)   applications for consents and, possibly, details of responses received as a result of consultation;
(ii)   consents, licences etc, with details of their conditions;
(iii)   details of variations, revocations and similar notices;
(iv)   records of monitoring data concerning licensed premises and processes;
(v)   information relating to any appeals (*e.g.* against refusal of any consent etc);
(vi)   details of convictions for offences under the statute concerned.

In all cases registers are open to public inspection at reasonable hours free of charge. A reasonable charge may be made for copies of documents.

The value of information

An individual lay member of the public or a special interest group will not usually be able to appreciate fully the operation of industrial premises or processes and the environmental impacts caused by them. However, properly used, the registers represent a major step forward in obtaining information toward such an understanding. Such information can be used for challenging proposals for new or modified development and, in particular, for checking on the performance of a process against given standards. The range of information now required to be placed on registers represents a potent weapon in the hands of the public, who are enabled not only to face up the operator of premises or processes with their responsibilities but also to challenge the performance of the regulators in ensuring compliance with the law and any consents and authorisations granted thereunder.

The different registers

(i) *Waste management*

Maintained by waste regulation authorities (usually county councils) and, in England, waste collection authorities, under the Environmental Protection Act 1990 (EPA 1990), Part II.

(ii) *Waste carriers*

Maintained by waste regulation authorities under the Control of Pollution (Amendment) Act 1989 and the Controlled Waste (Registration of Carriers and Seizure of Vehicles) Regulations 1991 (SI 1991/1624).

(iii) *Integrated pollution and local authority pollution control*

Maintained by HMIP and local authorities under section 20 of EPA 1990 and regulation 15 of the Environmental Protection (Applications, Appeals and Registers) Regulations 1991 (SI 1991/507). In the case of Part A prescribed processes, copies of the integrated pollution control (IPC) entries are maintained for that area by the local authority (reg 16) and National Rivers Authority (NRA) regional offices. For Part B processes the information is held by the relevant local authority.

(iv) *Alkali etc Works Regulation Act 1906*

Maintained by HMIP centrally and regionally, but with copies held by local authorities for the area where the process is located (Control of Industrial Air Pollution (Registration of Works) Regulations 1989 (SI 1989/318)).

(v) *Water: discharge consents*

Maintained by the NRA regional offices under section 190 of the Water Resources Act 1991 and the Control of Pollution (Registers) Regulations 1989 (SI 1989/1160).

(vi) *Water: trade effluent consents*

Maintained by sewerage undertakers at their offices under section 196 of the Water Industry Act 1991.

(vii) *Water: resources, abstraction etc*

Maintained by the NRA under section 197 of the Water Resources Act 1991.

(viii) *Radioactive Substances Act 1993*

Maintained by HMIP under section 39 of that Act. Copies are also held by local authorities. Registers have been maintained only since January 1991 and do not deal with the registration made before then. See also DoE Circulars 21/90 and 22/92.

(ix) *Town and country planning*

Maintained by local planning authorities. A range of information concerning planning matters is entered mainly under the Town and Country Planning Act 1990, articles 27 and 28 of the Town and Country Planning (General Development) Order 1988 (SI 1988/1813), the Planning (Hazardous Substances) Regulations 1992 (SI 1992/656) and the Town and Country Planning (Control of Advertisements) Regulations 1992 (SI 1992/666).

(x) *Local land charges*

Maintained by district councils under the provisions of the Local Land Charges Act 1975 and the Local Land Charges Rules 1977. They will disclose, for example, information about statutory nuisances.

(xi) *Genetically modified organisms*

Maintained by the Secretary of State (via HMIP) under EPA 1990, Part VI. The range of information to be included is set out in section 122 of the Act and regulation 16 of the Genetically Modified Organisms (Contained Use) Regulations 1992 (SI 1992/3217) and regulations 17 and 18 of the Genetically Modified Organisms (Deliberate Release) Regulations 1992 (SI 1992/3280).

(xii) *Noise abatement zones*

Maintained by local authorities who have exercised powers of designation under section 63 of the Control of Pollution Act 1974 (s 64 and the Control of Noise (Measurement and Registers) Regulations 1976 (SI 1976/37).

(xiii) *Atmospheric pollution*

Maintained by local authorities under Part V of the Clean Air Act 1993.

(xiv) *Litter control*

Maintained by principal litter authorities (*i.e.* all local authorities) (EPA 1990, ss 86 and 95).

(xv) *Chemical release inventory*

Compiled by HMIP from public register information held by that authority in respect of radioactive substances and prescribed processes subject to control under Part I of EPA 1990.

Environmental Information Regulations 1992

The Environmental Information Regulations (SI 1992/3240) implement the Directive on Freedom of Access to Information on the Environment (90/313/EEC). The regulations are wide-ranging and refer to "any" information concerning a variety of matters. For the information to be accessible it must be held by certain types of bodies defined as "relevant persons". In the main, this description encompasses all public authorities and can include some private bodies who have public-type responsibilities (*e.g.* the water and sewerage companies).

A person who wishes to obtain information from a relevant person must simply make a request for the release of the data. The relevant person is obliged to respond to that request.

Local authorities' meetings

In general, local authorities must allow public access to their proceedings and to the relevant papers. See Part VA and Schedule 12A of the Local Government Act 1972. The terms on which information is available are set out in section 100H of that Act.

Exempted information

It is important to note that there will be some circumstances, albeit limited, when the public will not be able to gain access to information. There are two main occasions when access may be denied. First, the operator of a process or owner of premises may make a claim for confidentiality of information supplied on the grounds that they wish to protect commercial or industrial secrets. For the most part this claim needs to be supported by evidence to the regulator (on a confidential basis). If the claim is supported, whether by the regulator or, on appeal, by the Secretary of State, the information to be protected is excised from the register. Information may also be excluded from registers where it affects national security. The provisions whereby exclusion is secured will vary depending upon the relevant statutory provision (but see, for example, sections 21 and 22 of EPA 1990).

Contents of Chapter 12

Chapter 12
Liabilities and Remedies

Introduction

For the most part the control of pollution and the maintenance of environmental protection is based upon a system of statute law, that is a succession of statutory requirements. Responsibility for enforcement rests with bodies which are creations of Central or Local Government. However, increasingly in recent times policing bodies are being established, placed more remotely from ministerial control. The most obvious example of this is the National Rivers Authority (NRA) established by the Water Act 1989 and there are plans to transform Her Majesty's Inspectorate of Pollution (HMIP) and the NRA into an environment agency. This agency would also take on the responsibilities of the waste regulation authorities under Part II of the Environmental Protection Act 1990 (EPA 1990). Legislation for this purpose is expected during 1994/95.

Thus, an individual's present main route of remedy is likely to be by complaint to the responsible authority, be it the NRA, HMIP or local government officer. The procedures set out in Parts I and II of this book represent the most straightforward and, possibly, the cheapest remedy. Indeed, proceedings ultimately resulting in action by the courts have tended to exclude the common man as primary participant. Frequently there was essentially no opportunity to proceed for breach of statutory responsibility against a polluter otherwise than via the route described above.

Civil procedures

The whole raft of formal criminal procedure should not obscure the fact that civil remedies exist in common law and increasingly are enshrined in the more modern legislation. Such legislation reflects greater public demand to the included in the whole process of value judgments about pollution control. Both the Water Resources Act 1991 and EPA 1990 have enlarged the responsibilities of industrial processors and other holders of authorisations to reveal, subject to certain protections, a considerable amount of detail about their activities and their environmental performance. Registers of consents, the results of monitoring and other information will now be readily available for inspection by members of the public who will have a right to take detailed particulars. Furthermore, restrictions on independent action for criminal sanctions against polluters are being withdrawn gradually, to the extent that "class" actions (*e.g.* proceedings taken by bodies formed by persons with closely related views, such as Friends of the Earth or Greenpeace), may be relatively common in the future.

Liabilities under common law

It would be inappropriate in a book of this type to examine in detail the law of trespass, nuisance or negligence which will be at the forefront of any practitioner's mind when considering the remedies open to a client. Suffice it to say that it would be obvious to a practitioner that where there is some interference from an external source with the beneficial use of premises occupied by the plaintiff or some physical injury to his premises or his property, or to himself, then an action in tort will lie. It is also obvious that the rule in *Rylands* v *Fletcher* (1868) LR 3 HL 330 will have application in many cases, although this has been modified recently (see *Cambridge Water Co* v *Eastern Counties Leather* [1994] 1 A11 ER 53).

Remedies at common law

Remedies will be available to a plaintiff along the same lines as those available to him in any action for trespass, nuisance and/or negligence. Such remedies will include the right to an injunction and/or damages. It may also include, where he wishes to proceed against a statutory authority, an "administrative" remedy such as *mandamus* or *certiorari*.

There now follows a brief examination of civil liability and remedies by reference to individual codes.

It is a defence to a common law action in nuisance that statutory authority exists. However, that authority must be certain, in so far as it authorises the commission of a nuisance (*Allen* v

Gulf Oil Refining Limited [1981] AC 101). The source of much guidance in regard to the law of nuisance by pollution of the atmosphere is the case of *Sturges* v *Bridgman* (1879) 11 Ch D 852. The standard of air pollution control by process operators will vary depending on the circumstances, in particular the neighbourhood and the ambient air quality. The following cases serve to clarify the extent to which the courts will go in dealing with nuisance claims and in awarding damages: *Walter* v *Selfe* (1852) 19 LTOS 308 (smoke); *Halsey* v *Esso Petroleum Co Ltd* [1961] 2 A11 ER 145 (noxious smells); *West* v *Bristol Tramways* [1908] 2 KB 14 (fumes).

The tort of negligence may be a relevant basis for a claim in certain circumstances (*Tutton* v *AD Walker Ltd* [1985] 2 A11 ER 757 and *Tysoe* v *Davies* [1984] RTR 88).

Action based upon statutory liability

The EPA 1990, Part I provides a strong basis for actions in negligence, in those cases where failure to comply with the statutory requirements is proved. Practitioners will be readily assisted by the publicity requirements of the Act (see ss 20–22 (public registers)). Again, the correct basis of approach for a potential plaintiff is to seek relief under the law of nuisance. Matter escaping from a defendant's land is likely to give rise to an action in nuisance, possibly by virtue of the rule in *Rylands* v *Fletcher* (1868) LR 3HL 330. Both the common law and the rule may be appropriate particularly to those cases where noxious waste material has been deposited on a defendant's land, thereby causing offensive smells or other wind-borne or water-borne deterioration of the plaintiff's property. An action in damages might lie together in certain circumstances with the right to an injunction. See also *Leakey* v *National Trust* [1980] 1 A11 ER 17; *Smith* v *Great Western Railway* (1926) 42 TLR 391.

The case of *Cambridge Water Company* v *Eastern Counties Leather* [1994] 1 A11 ER 53 was important in the sense that it confirmed that actions in nuisance and under the rule in *Rylands* v *Fletcher* will succeed only where the defendant can be shown reasonably to have foreseen the consequences of his action which caused the nuisance. Note also that a planning permission may cause a change in the character of a locality and, as a consequence, whether the harm is a nuisance or not must be judged by reference to that change of character (*Gillingham Borough Council* v *Medway (Chatham) Dock Co Limited* [1992] 3 All ER 923.

General note on common law remedies for individuals

The plaintiff would normally seek a remedy in nuisance by action for damages and an injunction will apply, particularly in those cases where a nuisance is likely to happen again. The Attorney-General may be prevailed upon to take proceedings for an injunction to prevent recurrence of public nuisance but a prior requirement would be that a large number of potential plaintiffs must be affected (see *Attorney-General* v *PYA Quarries Ltd* [1957] 2 QB 169).

Practitioners should also take into account *Gouriet* v *Union of Post Office Workers* [1978] AC 435. This House of Lords' case established that an action for an injunction to restrain an anticipated breach would be available to a private person only in circumstances where special harm or damage to some private right was proved.

Attention is also drawn to the right of private persons to bring summary proceedings for statutory nuisance under section 82 of EPA 1990 and, in regard to litter, similar provisions in section 91.

Water pollution

A riparian owner has a common law right to receive water in any stream or river, on or adjacent to his property, without harm to its natural condition. No proof of damage is required where harm arises, for example to livestock or other consumers (see *Young* v *Bankier Distillery Ltd* [1893] AC 691). The pollution of underground water will also be actionable in common law, for example by the dumping of waste by the defendant on adjacent land which then pollutes underground resources flowing on to the plaintiff's land. Note, however, that the plaintiff must establish that the defendant could reasonably foresee the connection between the dumping of the waste and the pollution of the resources.

It would appear that a statutory right to pollute (*e.g.* by ss 88 and 89 of the Water Resources Act 1991), is no defence to civil proceedings.

Restriction on right to prosecute

Under the Public Health Act 1936, section 298 there exists a restriction on any right to prosecute without the written consent of the Attorney-General. For such consent to be granted the applicant must be the party aggrieved (*i.e.* have a genuine grievance), or the local authority who have the enforcement powers.

Control of Pollution Act 1974

Section 88 of the Control of Pollution Act 1974 provides for civil liability for contravention of section 3(3), to the extent that where any damage is caused by poisonous, noxious or polluting waste deposited on land then, in so far as an offence has been created under section 3(3), the defendant is also liable specifically in civil law. The section overcomes the difficulty which would otherwise arise under section 105 of the Act, which restricts the extent to which an offence under the Act can be actionable as a civil remedy.

Water abstraction

It is only necessary to state here that an unlawful interference with the supply of surface or underground water to the extent that a plaintiff's right to abstract is detrimentally affected provides a civil action in tort against the person responsible. This is an extremely well-documented branch of the law of tort and practitioners are referred to standard textbooks on the subject.

Right of action against the NRA

The Water Resources Act 1991 contains a useful provision in circumstances where a licensed abstractor of water has suffered as a result of the breach of the duty imposed by section 39 of the Act. Subject to certain conditions and restrictions there is a right of action against the NRA under section 60 where the NRA is in breach of the duty to protect the right of an abstractor who has been granted a licence and who seeks to abstract in accordance with his licence and the conditions imposed. If the NRA has taken any action which it can be established derogates from a previous protected right then it is in breach of duty and may be proceeded against in respect of that breach. Circumstances such as this are most likely to arise where the NRA has granted a second or subsequent abstraction right which interferes with the earlier authorisation.

Statutory provision for civil liability

In some circumstances statute will modify normal civil liability rules. An example of this is in section 70 of the Water Resources Act 1991. Except in so far as the Act provides expressly, restrictions on abstraction, impounding and construction of wells or boreholes are not to be construed (i) as providing any right of action in any civil proceedings, or (ii) derogating from any right of action or other remedy (whether civil or criminal) in proceedings instituted otherwise under that part of the Act.

Appendix A
General List of IPC Processes Intended to be the Subject of Central (HMIP) Control

Gasification
Carbonisation
Combustion
Petroleum

Incineration
Chemical recovery
Chemical waste treatment
Waste-derived fuel

Cement and lime
Asbestos
Mineral fibres
Glass
Ceramic

Petrochemical
Organic chemical
Acids
Chemical fertiliser
Pharmaceutical

Halogens
Chemical fertiliser
Bulk chemical storage

Inorganic chemical
Pesticide

Iron and steel
Non-ferrous

Paper and pulp
Di-isocyanate
Tar and bitumen
Coating
Printing ink and coating
Dyestuffs
Timber
Animal and vegetable treatment

NB: This is intended to be a general list and readers are advised to examine in detail the full definitions of the processes prescribed for IPC control. See the Environmental Protection (Prescribed Processes and Substances) Regulations 1991 (SI 1991/472), as amended (see p 103). See also HMIP Guidance Note, "Integrated Pollution Control: A Practical Guide".

Appendix B
General List of Processes the Subject of Local Authority Air Pollution Controls

1.1 Gasification

(a) odorising natural gas or LPG
(b) blending odorant
(c) refining natural gas

1.3 Combustion

(a) boiler 20–50 MW
(b) gas turbine 20–50 MW
(c) waste oil up to 3 MW

2.1 Iron and steel

(a) electric arc furnace less than seven tonnes
(b) cupola, rotary furnace and other furnaces
(c) refining, making of iron, steel or ferrous alloys where air or oxygen used
(d) de-sulphurisation of iron, steel, ferro-alloy
(e) degreasing and other foundry operations, casting 50 tonnes or more

2.2 Non-ferrous metals

(a) aluminium
(b) copper/brass
(c) zinc
(d) scrap
(e) galvanizing
(f) foundry operations
(g) other non-ferrous
(h) metal decontamination
(i) calcined bauxite

3.1 Cement and lime

(a) cement handling/blending
(b) lime

3.2 Asbestos

3.4 Mineral

(a) crushing, grinding of designated minerals or products, coal, coke
(b) screening, grading, mixing coal, coke
(c) loading, unloading, coal, coke
(d) crushing, grinding, screening, bricks, tiles or concrete
(e) coating road stone
(f) loading, unloading, storing fuel ash

"Designated mineral" includes clay, sand, natural occurring minerals (except coal or lignite), metallurgical slag, boiler or furnace ash from coal etc, by-product gypsum.

3.5 Glass

(a) glass manufacture
(b) polishing
(c) glass frit

3.6 Ceramic

4.3 Acid processes

4.9 Storage of chemicals

5.1 Incinerators (small)

6.2 Di-isocyanates

6.3 Tar and bitumen

6.5 Coating

6.6 Coating manufacture

(a) ink
(b) powder
(c) other material

6.7 Timber

(a) manufacture
(b) chemical treatment

6.8 Processes involving rubber

(a) mixing, milling, blending of natural rubber or synthetic organic elastomers where carbon black used
(b) conversion to finished product

6.9 Animal and plant treatment

NB: This is a general list and readers are advised to examine in detail the full definitions of prescribed processes.

Appendix C
The Meaning of BATNEEC*

BATNEEC (or formulations which are equivalent in meaning) is gaining increasing currency in international standards relating to environmental protection. The most notable documents are the EC Air Framework Directive (84/360/EEC) and the EC Dangerous Substances Directive (76/464/EEC) and daughter Directives. The EC Directives use the term "best available technology". The Environmental Protection Act 1990 (EPA 1990) uses the term "best available techniques". "Techniques" are intended to include technology, but in addition to hardware are intended to include operational factors.

All processes prescribed under Part I of EPA 1990 are subject to the BATNEEC requirements. In general terms what is BATNEEC for one process is likely to be BATNEEC for a comparable process. However, in each case it is, in practice, for the enforcing authority (subject to appeal to the Secretary of State) to decide what is BATNEEC for the individual process and it will take into account variable factors such as configuration, size and other individual characteristics of the process in doing so. In the last resort the courts could overturn a decision if it was manifestly unreasonable. For reasons discussed later in this Appendix it will usually be necessary to have a general working definition of BATNEEC for the guidance of inspectors in the field, of the operators of scheduled processes and of the Secretary of State in determining appeals or in issuing directions to the Chief Inspector and to local authorities.

It should always be borne in mind that BATNEEC is one feature of a complex of objectives set out in section 7 of EPA 1990 which must be achieved in determining an application. In deciding an application no release can be tolerated which constitutes a recognised health hazard, either in the short term or long term.

In reducing the emissions to the lowest practicable amount, account needs to be taken of local conditions and circumstances, both of the process and the environment, the current state of

* Best available techniques not entailing excessive cost.

knowledge and the financial implications in relation to capital expenditure and revenue cost.

BAT

It is necessary to construe the words "best available techniques" separately and together.

"Techniques" embraces both the process used and how the process is operated. The word should be taken to mean the concept and design of the process, the components of which it is made up and the manner in which they are connected together to make the whole. It should also be taken to include matters such as staff numbers, working methods, training, supervision and manner of operating the process.

"Available" should be taken to mean procurable by any operator of the class of process in question. It does not imply that the technology is in general use, but it does require general accessibility. It does not imply that sources outside the UK are "unavailable"; nor does it not imply a multiplicity of sources. If there is a monopoly supplier the technique counts as being available provided that any and all operators can procure it.

"Best" must be taken to mean most effective in preventing, minimising or rendering harmless polluting emissions. On this definition, there may be more than one set of techniques that achieves the same degree of effectiveness (*i.e.* there may be more than one "best" technique. It implies that the technology effectiveness has been demonstrated.

NEEC

"Not entailing excessive cost" needs to be taken in two contexts, depending on whether it is applied to new processes or to existing processes.

The presumption will be that best available techniques will be used, but that presumption can be modified by economic considerations where it can be shown that the costs of applying best available techniques would be excessive in relation to the environmental protection to be achieved. If, for instance, one technology reduces the emission of a polluting substance by 90% and another reduces the emissions by 95% but at four times the cost, it may be a proper judgment to hold that because of the small benefit and the great cost the second technology would entail excessive cost. If the emissions were particularly dangerous, on the other hand, it may be proper to judge that the additional cost was not excessive.

EXISTING PROCESSES

In applying NEEC to BAT for existing processes we are concerned essentially with the timing of the upgrading of old processes to new standards. We are guided to some extent by Articles 12 and 13 of the Air Framework Directive.

Article 13, which applies to processes existing prior to 1987, requires certain factors to be taken into account.

"In the light of an examination of developments as regards the best available technology and the environmental situation, the Member States shall implement policies and strategies, including appropriate measures, for the gradual adaptation of existing plants belonging to the categories given in Annex 1 to the best available technology, taking into account in particular:

- the plant's technical characteristics,
- its rate of utilisation and length of its remaining life,
- the nature and volume of polluting emissions from it,
- the desirability of not entailing excessive costs for the plant concerned, having regard in particular to the economic situation of undertakings belonging to the category in question."

Article 12, which is concerned with keeping authorisations for existing processes up to date with respect to technological developments, sets out less extensive guidelines.

Emission standards

Clearly, BATNEEC may be expressed in technological terms (*i.e.* a requirement to employ specified hardware). However, given the definition of "best" above, it may also be expressed in terms of emission standards. Having identified the best technology and the emission values it is capable of producing, it would be possible to express BATNEEC as a performance standard, *i.e.* that technology which produces emission standards of X or better, where X are the values yielded by the identified BATNEEC. BATNEEC normally should be expressed in these terms in order to avoid the risk of constraining the development of cleaner technology or of restricting operators' choice of means to achieve a given standard.

The promulgation of BATNEEC

In each individual case the Chief Inspector or the local authority must decide what is BATNEEC and translate it into requirements in the conditions of the authorisation. There must, however, be consistency across the board. Individual inspectors should not be required to "re-invent the wheel" each time they determine an application for an authorisation. Process operators and, indeed, the public, will require an assurance that BATNEEC is being applied in a rational and consistent way. That dictates that the process of arriving at BATNEEC must be open and explicit. It is proposed to convey this information through the medium of published guidance to HMIP inspectors and to local authorities on the application of integrated pollution regulation or air pollution control (including BATNEEC factors) for classes of process. Where guidance is issued by the Secretary of State it must be taken into account by the enforcing authority in determining an application.

Openness

IPC is an open and explicit system of control. Guidance will give due consideration to the opinions of those who are being regulated and will be subject to consultation with the public as represented by interested bodies. It follows that guidance relating to the specification of BATNEEC and the timetable of application to existing processes will be preceded by consultation with representatives of the operators of the category of processes involved and, at a suitable point in time, the public more generally. The coverage of the guidance should be comprehensive, and subject to some form of publicly available programme. This is particularly relevant to the orderly implementation of Part I of EPA 1990. Process operators will have notice of the order and time-scale in which they will be brought into the system and be provided with the rationale for the priorities set.

Appendix D
I. Application for Authorisation under IPC

Her Majesty's Inspectorate of Pollution
The Environmental Protection Act 1990, section 6(3)

I Applicant's details

Application No

Registered name and address of applicant: Post code:

Companies House Registration No

Address of process location: [if mobile process then principal place of business] Post code: National Grid reference:

Address to which invoices should be sent: Post code:

Payment method: cheque/direct debit/payable order/other (please specify) . . . .
Payment by credit card not acceptable

Amount attached to application:

Local district council area in which
premises are located:
(if mobile process then local district council of principal place of business)

Waste regulation authority area:

Sewerage undertakers:

Are there any plans to discharge to controlled waters?

| Yes/No |

Are there any details you consider need to be covered by commercial confidentiality? If YES then please see the attached guidance note which details the procedures you must follow.

Please enclose copies of any consents/agreements/authorisations, etc that are currently held in respect to releases of substances from this process to the environment.

Please list below any copies or additional information enclosed with this application form:

Is this an application for a mobile process?   Yes/No

2 Applicant's declaration

I hereby declare that all information contained in this application is, to the best of my knowledge, correct.

Signed

Date

Note: it is an offence under section 23(h) of the Act to provide false or misleading information

Schedule reference no

Components contained within process (see guidance note):

Total number of components:

Section 2   Process information

1 State the category and purpose of the process.

2 Identify the prescribed substances involved in the process and any other substances which might cause harm if released into any environmental medium.

3 Describe briefly the process and the techniques that will ensure that the

pollution potential of the process is minimised including the process controls and the handling and storage of process materials.

4 Describe the pollution abatement plant that will be used for reducing the release of prescribed substances to a minimum and rendering harmless any other substances which might cause harm.

5 What contingency is available to cope with the breakdown or planned maintenance of plant?

6 Describe how the abatement plant copes with the full range of operating circumstances of the plant.

7 State whether the process will be operated continuously and give details of the staff employed to control the process.

8 Does this proposal constitute a commitment to the use of "best available techniques" (BAT)? Answer yes or no.

If no, set out the argument in support of the case that alternative techniques would entail excessive costs.

9 Give appropriate details if this application takes into account any plans, directions or prescriptions by the Secretary of State.

Section 3   Releases

1 Detail the release points and quantities of substances set out in section 2.2 above for which authorisation is sought during the operation of the process:

(i)   to the air;
(ii)   to the water.

2 What is the consequence of the release of these substances taking into account local circumstances? Give references for any assessment factors used.

3 Describe the other wastes which will be generated and state for which wastes an off-site treatment or disposal route will be sought and whether it has been secured. Is the pollution which may be caused to the environment from the permitted disposal of such wastes sensitive to any of the factors associated with the process on the site? What is the requirement to store such wastes on site prior to disposal?

4 Summarise briefly how the design and operation of this process will achieve the requirement to "minimise the pollution to the environment taken as a whole by the releases having regard to the best practicable environmental option available as respects the substances which may be released".

5 What research if any is being carried out or sponsored by the company in the context of BAT to further reduce the creation of wastes, limit the release of polluting substances and assess the impact of those that are released?

Section 4 Compliance

The applicant will be required as a condition of authorisation to make and implement adequate arrangements to demonstrate compliance with the conditions of the authorisation. This section is for the Company to propose how it could demonstrate compliance with possible authorisation conditions on:

(i)   feedstocks;
(ii)   process parameters;
(iii)   performance of pollution abatement plant;
(iv)   emission monitoring or sampling;
(v)   environmental sampling;
(vi)   analytical procedures;
(vii) quality assurance plans;
(viii) record keeping.

Reference should be made to British Standards Institute and other accepted procedures wherever possible.

If there is insufficient space on the application form please continue on separate sheets.

2. Certificate of Authorisation

Her Majesty's Inspectorate of Pollution
Environmental Protection Act 1990

ERNEST NONESUCH, CERTIFICATE OF AUTHORISATION

Ref No

The Chief Inspector, Her Majesty's Inspectorate of Pollution, in accordance with section   of the [Act] has determined the application dated
[and further information date   ] from Ernest Nonesuch plc

Registered office   No

and authorises this Company to carry on the process(es) as detailed in the application being a process(es) prescribed in Part A of Regulations made under [Section 2(1) of the Act] namely

at the premises occupied by the Company at   within the District of   in the County of   subject to the process controls and release limits set out in the schedule and the further conditions and limitations set out in pages   attached.

Signed _____

A person authorised to sign on behalf of the Chief Inspector

Dated the _____

Schedule

I Process controls [e.g.]

Parameters	Restriction
Temperature	1110˚C ± 25˚C
Throughput	> 25 tonnes/hr
Feedstocks	> 1 ppm Codmium

2 Releases to air

Releases of substance by specified outlets (OS ref)
nominated stock   substance   max concentration   max per [day]

3 Releases of prescribed substances to surface waters

nominated off-site routes (*e.g.* outfall, sewer, etc) (OS ref   )

4 Transfer of wastes containing prescribed substances other than for deposit including:

(i)   explanation;
(ii)   waste treatment (liquid);
(iii) waste conditioning.

Further conditions and limitations

I Process plants

The Company shall only carry out the authorised processes in those process units and plants and in those parts of the site detailed in the applications. Without prejudice to the general condition in [section 7(4) of the Act] the process shall be carried out so that the generation of waste [and the release of substances] are minimised and so that the parameters detailed in the schedule are complied with. In addition the Company shall [ensure that   ].

2 Containment of substances

The Company shall make and implement appropriate arrangements to ensure that raw materials, process intermediates, products and wastes are contained as described in the application and that any releases are only via nominated routes detailed in the schedule. In addition the Company shall:

[spray/cover stocks of raw materials etc]
[precautions during transfer]

3 Treatment and release of gaseous substances

The Company shall make and implement adequate arrangements to collect and treat [process gases] [gases mists and dusts] and ensure that it shall not release any substances to air except by those means detailed in the application and in accordance with the limits detailed in the schedule. In addition, the Company shall [ensure that emissions shall be colourless and free from droplets].

4 Treatment and release of liquid substances

The Company shall make and implement adequate arrangements to collect and treat liquid process arising as described in the application and that it shall not discharge any treated effluent except by those routes and in accordance with the limits detailed in the schedule. In addition, the Company shall: [ensure that   ].

5 Conditioning of process wastes

The Company shall make and implement adequate arrangements to condition [process] [incinerate] wastes as described in the application. In addition the Company shall [ensure that   ].

6 Demonstration of compliance

[Before commencement of the process the Company shall make available to any nominated Inspector copies of the arrangements required by this authorisation.] [The Company shall prepare a document to the satisfaction of the Chief Inspector specifying the means employed to ensure compliance with this authorisation. Thereafter, the Company shall obtain his written approval before making any changes to the means as specified in the document.]

(1) SAMPLING AND TESTING

The Company shall:

(i)   take and analyse such samples of substances which may be released as are necessary for the purpose of this authorisation;

(ii)   take and analyse such samples of substances which may be released and conduct other tests and surveys as the Chief Inspector may from time to time require;

(iii)   make and keep a record of such analysis test or survey;

(iv)   retain or despatch samples of substances which may be released as directed by the Chief Inspector.

(2) RECORDS AND PROVISION OF INFORMATION

The Company shall:

(i)   make and keep a record of such process parameters as may be necessary to demonstrate compliance with this authorisation and in a manner approved by the Chief Inspector in writing;

(ii)   make and keep a record of substances released as may be necessary to demonstrate compliance with this authorisation and in a manner approved by the Chief Inspector in writing;

(iii)   keep the records required to be made in a manner and for a period and in a place approved by the Chief Inspector in writing, and ensure that any amendment to the records leaves the original entry clear and legible.

7   Special conditions relating to limits or plans set by the Secretary of State

8   Provision of information for the public register

[Is this required as an authorisation condition?]

9   Interpretation etc

10   *Subject to the condition in section 6 above this authorisation shall come into effect on*

Appendix E
A Note on the Influence of European Community Legislation

Introduction

There is a strong impetus in the pace of legislation flowing from the environment programme of the European Community. It must be concluded that this is inevitably having a profound effect upon the Government's parliamentary programme and the consequences for business and industry in the United Kingdom. The two major statutes dealing with environment standards, the Water Resources Act 1991 and the Environmental Protection Act 1990 accommodate and, to a certain extent, anticipate what has emerged and will develop from Brussels during the 1990s. The Government's environment White Paper, "This Common Inheritance", deals comprehensively with what it perceives are its responsibilities within the context of Europe. Paragraph 3.8 sets out the approach:

> "The Government therefore believes that the Community's programme for the environment must be vigorous and forward-looking, tackling issues in ways which are consistent with the responsibilities we owe to future generations and which encourage people to use Europe's natural resources in sustainable ways. The polluter must pay wherever possible. Action must be based on the best science available, but scientific uncertainty must not be an excuse for delay where there are clear threats of damage that could be serious or irreversible. As in Britain, we must weigh the costs of proposals for action carefully against the benefits and try to make sure that priority is given to measures that give the best and most urgent results most cost-effectively. It is the Government's aim to make sure that the standards that the Community sets do their job effectively, and that they do not put British people and firms at an unfair disadvantage; and to see that all EC policies – not just those on the environment itself – take environmental questions properly into account."

The basis of the Common Market environment programme

The legislation programme of the European Community is in the form mainly of Directives and regulations. The basis of environmental Directives and Regulations is (since 1 July 1987) Article 130R of the revised Treaty of Rome, brought into force so far as the United Kingdom is concerned by the Single European Act 1986. Article 130R2 requires that "action by the Community relating to the environment shall be based on the principles that preventative action should be taken, that environmental damage should, as a priority, be rectified at source, and that the polluter should pay. The article also acknowledges the far reaching and all pervading influence of environmental protection in that it requires that protection to be a component of the Community's other policies". This has been echoed by the UK Government in the White Paper.

The distinction between Directives and regulations is often not understood fully. Directives are, in effect, an instruction to Member States to achieve the objectives of the Directive in question. How they do this is a matter for individual States, although achievement is usually by legislation or other codes. Partly because of slow progress by certain Member States in implementing Directives, there is now some emphasis on the power of the regulation. Once confirmed, regulations passed by the Community bind individuals and organisations within each Member State directly. This means that no further legislation is required within Member States, although this frequently follows as a matter of consistency and clarification. Enforcement remains the responsibility of the Member State, although overall policing of the performance rests with the Community and, increasingly in the future, with the European Environment Agency (EEA).

Established by Council Regulation 1210/90, the EEA's present role is the assembly (through national agencies) of information. This is, of course, a restricted role and one which has drawn some criticism from environmental organisations throughout Europe. It is certainly a very tentative start and is no doubt a reflection of hesitancy on the part of Member States' governments about reassigning enforcement responsibilities (and thereby political influence thereon) to what would be a much more independent body. A better argument for the United Kingdom and some of the other Member States is that each already has in place a very well-developed regime of regulation, and duplication of this would be highly undesirable. The role of the EEA is due to be reviewed after two years and it seems inevitable that members of the European Commission will see a stronger range of duties being devolved, including the monitoring of the implementation of Community environmental legislation.

Directives already approved by the EC

Listed below are some of the more significant Directives and regulations concerning environmental matters (see p 167).

New European initiatives

(i)   *Amendment of the "Framework" Waste Directive 75/442/ EEC.* The amended Directive, published in 1988, is now approved as Council Directive 91/156/EEC. Its scope includes a stricter definition of waste, a greater emphasis on the encouragement of recycling, the strengthening of controls on disposal sites, an injunction to Member States to become self-sufficient in waste disposal capacity, to contribute towards an integrated network of disposal installations and to require registration of waste carriers and brokers.

(ii) *Hazardous waste.* This revised Directive was adopted in 1991 (91/689/EEC). It replaces the Directive on toxic and dangerous waste (78/319/EEC). The function of this Directive is to define hazardous waste in more detail, strengthen controls and extend them to producers, controlling collection, transport and temporary storage and requiring hazardous waste disposal plans. It does not apply to domestic waste.

(iii) *Landfill Directive.* This Directive has been the subject of hard negotiation. It seeks to identify three types of landfill (a) hazardous waste, (b) municipal and non-hazardous waste and (c) inert waste. Originally, it sought to exclude certain wastes, including clinical wastes or liquids. Some Member States, including the United Kingdom, have not been happy with the definitions. Co-disposal of hazardous wastes, previously not permitted by the draft, has also been accommodated.

The Directive will also require that landfill is specifically to be rejected in ground water protection zones, nature protection zones and areas of high risk of floods, subsidence or inadequate hydro-geological conditions. There was a number of specific locational requirements, including minimum distances between the landfill and sensitive areas and resources (*e.g.* residences, water bodies etc). It is noticeable that in the later drafts of the Directive the specific minimum separation distances have been dropped in favour of a more general, pragmatic approach, but with landfilling standards in harmony from State to State. Landfill operators would be obliged to provide financial guarantees in respect of environmental liabilities and after-care. Environmental assessments will be required for all sites except sites dealing with inert wastes. Finally, the "polluter pays" principle is manifested in requirements that landfill charges must cover all operational costs and that a State waste management fund (no doubt with industry contribution) should be established to deal with damage from all waste disposal which is incapable of being dealt with by other means (*e.g.* through the licensing system). Negotiations continue.

(iv) *Carbon/energy tax.* A highly significant development of the European Commission's influence would be the adoption of a system of environment taxation. A proposed carbon/energy tax is favoured by a number of Member States, notably Germany and France, but deep reservations are expressed by the United Kingdom, Spain and Portugal. It is anticipated that any proposals approved will not bear directly on industry but on energy use in the domestic, transport and service sectors.

(v) *Air pollution.* Present EC initiatives now concentrate on more specific aspects of air pollution control. Negotiations are continuing in respect of a Directive on emissions from large combustion plant in the 50–100 MW sector and on integrated pollution prevention and control. This Directive is largely anticipated by Part I of the UK Environmental Protection Act 1990. Additionally, an EC regulation on ozone-depleting chemicals is in the final phases of approval and negotiations continue on a Directive to limit industrial emissions of volatile organic compounds (VOCs).

(vi) *Recycling.* The approach to recycling by the Commission has been largely on the basis of an attack on individual product areas. The first of these was in relation to "beverage containers" (85/339/EEC) which required Member States to establish recycling programmes, although these could be voluntary. However, there is a current proposal which may set minimum recycling targets. This relates to packaging and its waste.

(vii) Batteries containing mercury, lead or cadmium are the

subject of an agreed Directive. Recyclability will be the subject of compulsory labelling and an excess of mercury in batteries is banned as from the beginning of 1993 (91/157/EEC).

(viii) In capital expenditure terms, the most significant Directive is that dealing with standards and requirements for supply and treatment of municipal waste water (sewage). Estimates of the likely UK cost exceed £1.5 billion, may need to be spent over 10 years if the ambitious programme is to be met. It is to be borne in mind that simply the borrowing cost of this level of expenditure will exceed the current turnover of some water companies. The implications of the huge figures call into question the regular absence of any cost-benefit analysis of EC proposals. Tax and charge-payers in the United Kingdom may complain but the costs to Mediterranean States will be much greater. A reminder of the influence of Brussels could hardly be more stark.

EEC Legislation

WASTE ON LAND

1975 Council Directive on the Disposal of Waste Oils (75/439/EEC)

1975 Council Directive on Waste (75/442/EEC)

1976 Council Directive on the Disposal of PCBs (76/403/EEC)

1978 Council Directive on Toxic and Dangerous Waste (78/319/EEC)

1984 Council Directive on the Supervision and Control within the European Community of the Transfrontier Shipment of Hazardous Waste (84/631/EEC)

1986 Council Directive on the Protection of the Environment when Sewage Sludge is Used in Agriculture (86/278/EEC)

1991 Council Directive on Waste (91/156/EEC) replaces most of Directive 75/442/EEC

1993 Council Regulation 259/93 on the Supervision and Control of Shipments of Waste

1993 Commission Decision on a List of Waste (93/442/EEC)

POLLUTION OF INLAND WATERS

1973 Council Directive on Detergents (73/404/EEC)

1973 Council Directive on the Control of the Biodegradability of Anionic Surfactants (73/405/EEC)

1975 Council Directive on the Quality of Surface Water for Drinking (75/440/EEC)

1975 Council Directive on the Quality of Bathing Water (76/160/EEC)

1976 Council Directive on Pollution caused by the Discharge of Certain Dangerous Substances into the Aquatic Environment (76/464/EEC)

1978 Council Directive on the Quality of Fresh Waters Needed to Support Fish Life (78/659/EEC)

1979 Council Directive on the Quality Required of Shellfish Waters (79/923/EEC)

1979 Council Directive on the Protection of Groundwater against Pollution Caused by Certain Dangerous Substances (80/68/EEC)

1980 Council Directive on the Quality of Water for Human Consumption (80/778/EEC)

1991 Council Directive on Urban Waste Water Treatment (91/271/EEC)

1991 Council Directive concerning the Protection of Waters against Pollution Caused by Nitrates from Agricultural Sources (91/676/EEC)

ATMOSPHERIC POLLUTION

1970 Council Directive on Air Pollution by Motor Vehicles (70/220/EEC)

1975 Council Directive on the Sulphur Content of Certain Liquid Fuels (75/716/EEC)

1977 Council Directive on the Emission of Pollutants by Diesel Engines for Use in Tractors (77/537/EEC)

1980 Council Directive on Air Quality Limit Values for Sulphur Dioxide and Suspended Particulates (80/779/EEC)

1982 Council Directive on a Limit Value for Lead in the Air (82/884/EEC)

1984 Council Directive on the Combating of Air Pollution from Industrial Plants (84/360/EEC)

1985 Council Directive on Air Quality Standards for Nitrogen Dioxide (85/203/EEC)

1985 Council Directive on the Lead Content of Petrol (85/210/EEC)

1987 Council Directive on Measures to be Taken against the Emission of Gaseous Pollutants from Diesel Engines for Use in Vehicles (88/77/EEC)

1988 Council Regulation 3322/88 on Certain Chlorofluorocarbons and Halons which Deplete the Ozone Layer

1988 Council Directive on the Limitation of Emissions of Certain Pollutants into the Air from Large Combustion Plants (88/609/EEC)

1989 Council Directive on the Prevention of Air Pollution from New Municipal Waste Incineration Plants (89/369/EEC)

1989 Council Directive on the Reduction of Air Pollution from Existing Municipal Waste-Incineration Plants (89/429/EEC)

1991 Council Regulation of Substances that Deplete the Ozone Layer (91/594/EEC)

1992 Council Directive on Air Pollution by Ozone (92/73/EEC)

1993 Council Directive on Greenhouse Gas Emissions (93/389/EEC)

POLLUTION BY NOISE

1970 Council Directive on Noise from Motor Vehicles (70/157/EEC)

1978 Council Directive on Noise from Motorcycles (78/1015/EEC)

1978 Council Directive on Noise from Construction Plant and Equipment (79/113/EEC)

1979 Council Directive on Noise from Subsonic Aircraft (80/51/EEC)

DANGEROUS SUBSTANCES

1978 Council Directive prohibiting the Placing on the Market and Use of Plant Protection Products Containing Certain Active Substances (79/117/EEC)

1980 Council Directive amending the Directives laying down the Basic Safety Standards for the Health Protection of the General Public and Workers against the Dangers of Ionising Radiation (80/836/EURATOM)

1982 Council Directive on the Major Accident Hazards of Certain Industrial Activities (82/501/EEC)
1987 Council Regulation (Euratom) 3954/87 laying down Maximum Permitted Levels of Radioactive Contamination of Foodstuffs and of Feedingstuffs following a Nuclear Accident or Any Other Case of Radiological Emergency
1988 Council Regulation 1734/88 Concerning Export from and Import into the Community of Certain Dangerous Chemicals
1990 Commission Regulation (Euratom) 770/90 laying down Maximum Permitted Levels of Radioactive Contamination of Feeding Stuffs following a Nuclear Accident or Any Other Case of Radiological Emergency
1990 Council Directive on the Contained Use of Genetically Modified Micro-Organisms (90/219/EEC)
1990 Council Directive on the Deliberate Release into the Environment of Genetically Modified Organisms (90/220/EEC)
1991 Council Directive on Batteries and Accumulators concerning Certain Dangerous Substances (91/157/EEC)
1993 Council Directive on Minimum Requirements for Vessel Carrying Dangerous or Polluting Goods (93/75/EEC)

ENVIRONMENTAL IMPACT ASSESSMENT

1985 Council Directive on the Assessment of the Effects of Certain Public and Private Projects on the Environment (85/337/EEC)

MISCELLANEOUS

1990 Council Regulation 1210/90 on the Establishment of the European Environment Agency and the European Environment Information and Observation Network
1990 Council Directive on the Freedom of Access to Information on the Environment (90/313/EEC)
1992 Council Regulation 880/92 on Community Eco-Label Award Scheme

Appendix F
Further Reading

Garner & Harris, *Control of Pollution Encyclopedia* (Bartholomews).

Cross, *Encyclopedia of Environmental Health Law and Practice* (Sweet & Maxwell.

Halsbury's Laws of England, 4th ed (Butterworths).

Howarth, *The Law of the National Rivers Authority* (National Rivers Authority and Centre for Law in Rural Areas).

W Howarth, *Water Pollution Law* (Shaw & Sons).

John H Bates, *Water and Drainage Law* (Sweet & Maxwell).

Nigel Haigh, *EEC Environmental Policy and Britain* 2nd ed (Longman).

Clerk and Lindsell on Tort, (Sweet & Maxwell).

John Garbutt, *Waste Management Law – A Practical Handbook* (Chancery Law Publishing).

Paine, *Commercial Environmental Law and Liability* (Longman).

Index